Eyes of the Blind

EYES OF THE BLIND

BARTH HOOGSTRATEN

To order additional copies of this book, contact:
Xlibris Corporation
1-888-7-XLIBRIS
www.Xlibris.com
Orders@Xlibris.com

CONTENTS

To

Bets and Ann, who showed that being blind
is no barrier for extraordinary courage.

The people who kept their faith in the face
of death, the Jews.

The men and women in the occupied
countries who stood before the firing squads
because they had resisted the Nazi demon.

"We are blind, but that doesn't mean that we
can not be the same as other people".
Ann Frank

"We are normal people".
Bets Frank

Proceeds from the sale of *Eyes of the Blind*
will go to cancer research and the search of
light behind the unseeing eye.

Acknowledgements

I should like to thank my sister-in-law, Mieke Adama, for giving valuable insight into the work of the couriers during the occupation. Mieke was the leader of a group of ten couriers in Hilversum. I owe a primary debt to Sandra Luckow, who in her never-ending enthusiasm forced me to make this book from a collection of stories. My thanks also go to Cheryl Lopanik for her excellent copy editing. Editions of "Eigen Perk", the periodical of the Historical Society of Hilversum "Albertus Perk", formed an important source for writing Chapter 17, as was the booklet "Hilversum-Onderdrukking en Verzet, 1940-1945". And I am indebted to Mr Abraham van der Schuyt, the Editor of "Eigen Perk", for his advice and patient ear. Lastly, I should like to thank Geof and George Jenkins for their assistance with the cover.

THE COVER

Just like a simple pawn can win the game in chess,
could a determined man or woman beat a Nazi.

A blind chess player identifies a black piece by the small knob on its top.

Prologue

At the outbreak of World War II, the Netherlands declared its neutrality, but that didn't stop the German army from crossing the Dutch borders. Hours after the unprovoked invasion, an arrogant German ambassador delivered an ultimatum:

"We announce the deployment of an overwhelming German military force. Every resistance is useless. If you do not surrender it will result in the complete destruction of the country."

The German High Command—expecting surrender in a few hours—became furious when its troops met stiff resistance at all fronts. On that first day alone its air force lost one hundred forty planes. Nobody thought it possible for the Dutch resistance to last much longer, but the Germans were in a hurry. This little country of Holland tied down strong German forces much needed for the battle in France. On the 14th of May 1940, the Germans demanded an unconditional surrender before 4:30 PM that day; otherwise Rotterdam, which had been declared an open city, would be bombed. Treacherously the Luftwaffe began bombing the city three hours before the deadline. The entire center of Rotterdam was wiped out and the number of casualties ran in the thousands.

"Surrender or Utrecht will be flattened next," the German High Command announced. The fight was over, but the hatred against the Nazis for that cowardly bombing would endure. Queen Wilhelmina and her family barely escaped to England. The Dutch have always felt close to the Royal Family. Throughout the centuries the House of Orange had been a unifying force and the Germans were well aware of it. They immediately changed the names of all streets named after members of the Royal Family, forbade the wearing of anything orange, and eliminated all references to the House of Orange from schoolbooks.

They never quite succeeded. On June 29, 1940, the birthday of the German-born Prince Bernhard—who always wore a white carnation—numerous Dutchmen took to the streets with white carnations to honor him. Soon there weren't any live carnations available, so the townspeople made them from white paper. The Germans were helpless against this mass demonstration. On August 31, 1941, the citizens of Bussum woke up to find a towering factory chimney decorated from top to bottom with huge letters "Oranje Boven" (orange on top). It was the birthday of Queen Wilhelmina.

On April 29, 1943, the German High Command in Holland announced that all former officers and soldiers of the Dutch army had to report as prisoners of war. The official reason was that so many had joined the ever-increasing resistance, but in fact the Germans desperately needed the 300,000 men as slave laborers so that their own men would be freed for the armed forces. Holland went on strike. In retaliation, the Nazis immediately took prisoners at random and executed one hundred fifty. The strike lasted ten days, long enough for most of the Dutch soldiers to go underground.

"Onderduiker" (literally "one who ducks under"), became a new word soon after the German occupation began. It described the tens of thousands who had to live in hiding during the war, people who could no longer use their own name, sleep in their own bed or sit with their family at their own table . . . not knowing what might happen if they were caught. Concentration camp? Prison? Torture? The rifles of a Nazi execution squad? Those tens of thousands needed hiding places, food (already in very short supply) and false documents, all provided at great personal risks.

On September 17, 1944, the Dutch government-in-exile urged all employees of the railroads to go on strike. That day was the beginning of the battle of Arnhem of "A Bridge Too Far" fame. The entire railroad network came to a standstill, which lasted until the day all Holland was liberated, May 5, 1945. The price of the sacrifice paid by these workers was enormous, but it was simply one more heroic deed by a people fighting for freedom.

As in other occupied countries, Holland had its resistance fighters. They ran the illegal press, served as couriers, sabotaged strategic factories, smuggled downed allied pilots back to England, did intelligence work such as providing the allies with choice targets for bombing, and executed key collaborators and Nazi officials. Reichsmarshal Hermann Goering, the number two man in the Nazi hierarchy, once complained that "Of all the nations we have conquered, the Dutch are the most hostile." When caught, the people of Holland paid with the highest price, their life. Just before he was led away for his execution, one young Dutchman hastily scribbled these last words on the back of his cell door, "God, help my wife and children. I'll be all right."

About 2,800 Dutch men and women faced German firing squads. Untold thousands more died in prison and Nazi concentration camps. Holland lost more than two hundred thousand citizens, close to three per cent of the entire population at that time. Our Jews made up half of this number. The total came to 23 deaths per 1,000 citizens, three times higher than the losses in England. Not known is how many others died from hunger and disease. And how did we feel about it all? We did not bow our heads under the German yoke. The constant threat of the firing squads did not deter the resistance fighters. Despite the terror, the executions, and the constant

15

Nazi boot on their necks, the Dutch remained defiant, kept their heads up high and lived towards the day when the last German was thrown out. These feelings were never better expressed than in a poem written by a father after his daughter was arrested.

COURIER

Danger spied upon her from day to day
And every evening coming home,
It was a wonder that no harm had come
And the old house still welcomed her.

Every morning she faithfully put on the
Vest of the courier and mounted her bike.
The day full of tension and danger to meet,
At the end of the street she looked back once more.

The net tightens and even while still safe,
At every point of contact a trap may be found.
Oh, God, stand by her. Instead of friends
At the top of the stairs the face of the Nazi beast!

The car races through familiar streets,
Still full of bright memories from school,
How short – how long ago seems everything,
The car stops.... God.... Do not forsake me!

Like massive phantoms rise steep
Gray prison walls, stark windows with bars.
... High in the elm tree she hears the blackbird singing,
Yonder on the lake floats a sail aglitter.

17

A golden rim on Western horizon
A breeze wafting through early summer green
And with the hunger of her twenty years
She drinks – a single draft – God's beautiful world.

A small figure mere, she fades through the wall.
Heavy doors grind screeching to a close
But proudly she dares lift her head high
She did "her duty for God and for her country."

(Translated from het Contactorgaan van de
Landelijke Organisatie van Onderduikers)

1

Meeting The Sisters

It took me completely by surprise when she opened the front door of number 35 Rembrandt Avenue herself, because I had expected a maid to answer the doorbell.

"Bart?"

Her head tilted a bit to the right as she spoke and her lips parted in a hesitant, almost questioning smile as she looked at me. Yet, her eyes didn't meet mine. They were directed towards my right ear, just a little bit off target. My first impulse was to move my head so that I could meet her eyes, but I checked myself just in time. She stuck her hand out and I took it.

"Oh! You are taller than Jan," she said.

Again she surprised me. How on earth could she know that I was taller than my friend? I had yet to say a word, so it couldn't be by hearing where my voice came from.

"How do you know that?" I asked.

She laughed.

"When you took my hand it came from higher up than when Jan shakes my hand." At six feet one, I was four inches taller than Jan and she had already figured that out. At first glance, Miss Frank's eyes looked normal. They were shining, friendly, and even had some expression. It was only when she looked at me and her eyes didn't quite meet mine that I noticed the lack of focus. Jan, a fellow medical student, had told me about her blindness. For six months, he had driven

19

her on a bicycle for two, a tandem, to the Institute for the Blind in the nearby town of Huizen, where she was the principal piano teacher. But driving her back and forth between the institute and her house four days a week, while at the same time trying to keep up with his study had become too much for him and he had asked if I was interested in the job. It paid seven guilders a week and since I needed the money badly, I had agreed to meet Ms. Frank.

"Shall we go inside?"

She led the way through the hallway into the front room, walking without any hesitation and much faster than I anticipated.

"Please sit down. Would you like a cup of tea or a glass of lemonade?"

"Lemonade, please."

She spoke in the decisive manner of someone accustomed to giving orders. Authoritative but in a friendly sort of way, her voice was clear and pleasant. She left the room and that gave me a chance to look around. The room was dominated by a magnificent black grand piano in the right corner, near a wide front window. A rectangular piano stool was long enough to accommodate two persons. The piano was cluttered with thick, light brown books that didn't look like any of the books I had ever seen. A comfortable couch, a small chair and a coffee table occupied the left corner. Four throw pillows added color to the couch. Diagonally across from the piano was the fireplace with a built-in heating stove. Two easy chairs and a low, round table formed a pleasant setting in front of the stove. One chair had a little footstool. A large Persian rug covered most of the floor and smaller ones overlaid the two tables. A heavy vase, filled with heather in bloom, decorated the round table. The light blue flowers blended beautifully with the colors of the rug. Above the fireplace hung a silk multi-colored shawl, which was fixed in one corner with a large round clasp in the form of the sun, with beams radiating. The room was lit by two floor lamps, both with orange shades, a lamp fixture on the wall above the radio, and by a piano lamp. It was a warm, pleasant room. Piano music filtered down from upstairs.

She came back with a tray and two glasses of lemonade and I was again amazed by the ease with which she moved, so sure of herself. It was only when she momentarily felt for the edge of the round table before putting down the tray that it was noticeable that she was blind. Jan had warned me not to help her, but it was hard not to give a hand.

"My sister Bets will be downstairs any moment." She took charge again.

"My name is Anna Frank, but most people call me Annie, and my sister's name is Bets. We are blind, you know."

She laughed in short bursts, flinging her head upward and to the right in small, jerky motions.

"What did Jan tell you about driving me?"

"Actually, not much," I said.

"Well, four days a week I work at the Institute in Huizen and I need someone to drive me there."

Miss Frank—for some reason I never could call her Annie; she became Ann to me—explained what I was supposed to do if I accepted the job. I guessed her to be in her mid 50s. She was of average height and weight and kept a straight posture. Her face was strong, the mouth large, lips full. A good-sized nose was slightly out of kilter to the right. Two long wrinkles grooved a high forehead. Her short, early graying hair was parted on the left. She wore a gold necklace, a circle divided in three equal parts by lines that met in the center. It looked like the hood ornament of a Mercedes. Suddenly it occurred to me that I was looking at her in a way I would never look at someone who could see. I was being impolite without her knowing it, in a way taking advantage of her blindness.

The door flew open and a petite woman dashed in and clapped her hands together. "Is he here?" It was Bets. We

21

shook hands and she too remarked that I was tall. She sat on the edge of the chair with the footstool.

"Why don't you tell us something about yourself?" Ann said. "We only know that your name is Bart."

"Well, actually I spell it with an 'h' at the end, Barth."

"That's unusual, isn't it?" Bets asked.

"Yes, it is. My full name is Bartholomeus, but people always called me Bep and I didn't like that. So I changed it to Bart after I read a book entitled 'Bartje.' Do you know the book?"

"Yes we do," Ann said. "That was about the little farm boy, whose mother promised him leftover beans for supper instead of only potatoes. She forgot about her promise and when she insisted that he eat his potatoes, he ran away from home."

"And the title of the second book was 'Bart,' and I think there also was a third volume by the same author," Bets added.

"That's right and the title was 'Bart Seeks Happiness.' I added the "h" just to be different. Now, may I ask you something?"

"Sure, go ahead," Ann said.

"Who turned on the light?"

"I did."

"Is that because you knew that I was coming?"

"No, we always turn the light on when it gets dark."

"And how do you know when it is dark?"

"You have a lot of questions." This time it was Bets who answered. "We always know approximately what time it is and so we turn it on. And, before we go to bed, we turn it off."

"But how do you know that a light is still on?" Their answers only fed my curiosity.

"We just feel the warmth of the lamps. That's why we have no ceiling light in this room. We wouldn't be able to reach it." Ann chuckled. "But now it's our turn to ask some questions. How old are you?"

"I am eighteen. I am a medical student and . . . ."

"Yes, Jan told us," she interrupted. "Why do you want to be a doctor?"

"I really want to be surgeon ever since I was ten years old. You see, I was born with a tumor on my right ankle. It kept growing and when I was five years old it was so large that I could no longer wear a shoe. My Dad used to cut away the instep of a wooden shoe and that's how I got around, on wooden shoes. But that is a long story."

"No, no, no. We want to hear it all." Ann said emphatically. "That's the only way we can get a picture of you. It takes the place of seeing you."

"I want to hear it too," Bets said in eager anticipation. Her head was tilted up a little and to the left. I fetched the small chair and joined them at the round table.

"When I was six years old, the ankle had become so large that some boys began calling me names: 'Club- foot, club-foot, the red head has a club-foot'."

"Oh! You have red hair? How nice. I like red hair," Bets said. "But why did they call you names?"

I shrugged.

"Everybody always did, but mostly the boys in school. I was used to it."

"What else did they call you?" Ann asked.

"Oh, like, 'Hey, Redhead, did you sleep in a rusty bed?' or, ' Redhead did you drink too much coffee?' I don't even drink coffee and never knew what it had to do with the color of my hair."

"Did you fight them?" Bets said. She sounded feisty.

"Yes I did, but after a while I wizened up and refused to fight. Besides, they weren't used to my way of fighting. I would quickly take off my wooden shoes and threaten to hit them with it. Then they usually ran away. Sometimes, they

23

yelled at my sister and pulled her red hair, and that started the fighting all over again."

"Good for you," Ann said. "Did you fight all of them?"

"No, and that's just what is so strange about it. It was nearly always with the same boy. His hair was white and they called him 'Cheesehead.' They told him to fight me and for some reason he did, while they stood around yelling."

"Did you get a bloody nose?" Bets said.

"No, he tried all right, but my nose never bled. Anyway, when I was nine years old, the headmaster of our school told my mother that she should take me to a doctor. She did and a week later I was in the hospital."

"I've never been in a hospital," Bets said. "Did you have a nice room?"

"No, we were in a big ward where everything was white, except the floor. Two women were making beds when I came in. They wore long white dresses, all the way down to the floor. Their heads were covered with white wimples. Only their shoes were black. I later learned that they were nuns and that it was a Catholic hospital. The boy in the bed next to me and I were the only boys. The rest were grown men. That boy was about my age. I remember how pale he was and very thin and that he lay flat in bed all day. His pajamas were wrinkled, not like mine. I wore new pajamas, light blue ones, with some fancy embroidery around the buttons. "You'll need new pajamas when you go to the hospital," mother had said. Light blue pajamas, straight from the box. On the morning of my surgery the nun gave me a pill and that made me drowsy. Then they put me on a stretcher and took me for the nicest ride I ever had. Everything seemed to float and there were the sounds of voices and laughter far away. And that is the last thing I remember of the surgery. When I woke up, my father and uncle Henk stood at the foot of my bed, but all I could say was 'Hi' and I went right back to sleep. A week later, the sutures had to come out and I was scared because it always hurts when a bandage comes off and this was a big bandage."

"I had a bandage on my knee once and it was stuck when the head-mistress tried to take it off. It hurts," Bets interjected. She was listening intensely, her facial expressions changing constantly as I talked. She was vivacious, I thought. Ann, on the other hand, sat quietly, eyebrows slightly raised, studious.

"The doctor—his name was Huisman—came to my bed. Behind him a nun pushed a cart with instruments. 'Well young man, let's have a look at it.' Dr. Huisman had a pleasant voice. He started to take off the bandage and I tried not to tremble.

" 'You want to have a look?' he asked."

" 'Is it off?' My little voice asked."

"He laughed. 'Yes it is.' I hadn't even felt it. They had put some stuff on the wound before putting on the bandage and that had kept it soft."

Bets made a face. "That gives me the shivers."

"Oh, Bets, be quiet." Ann admonished her older sister.

"I slowly raised my head and looked. The incision was about six inches long, in a half circle, and there were many black sutures. But the big lump was gone. Two days later, the doctor removed about half of the sutures while I looked on. He only took out the ones that moved when he pulled on them. 'The others are not ripe yet,' he joked. The next morning, after Dr. Huisman had removed another suture, he said, 'Here, you do it.' And I did. I lifted the suture with a pair of tweezers just like I had seen him do it, cut it on one side with the scissors and then pulled it out from the other end. It worked and that's when I decided to become a surgeon."

"That doctor was a good psychologist," Ann said rather dryly.

"He knew it. He saw it in you," Bets said enthusiastically. Then, in a concerned voice, she said, "What happened to the other boy?"

25

"He died."

"His soul went up the ladder," she said quietly.

I didn't know what she meant by that and I didn't ask.

"Anyway, my family also adopted the idea of me becoming a doctor. Nobody in our family had ever gone to high school, let alone university, so it became some sort of a rallying point. 'Barth is going to be a doctor.' A family pride. But my parents couldn't afford the costs of high school, let alone medical school. The only way I could go through high school was with a scholarship, which paid for the tuition. I also received a scholarship for the university and worked for my dad during vacations. I bought second-hand books with the money I earned. And that's about it."

Their curiosity still wasn't satisfied and other questions came. "What kind of work does your father do?"

"My dad is a master bricklayer and master plasterer."

I was proud of my dad. He was one of only five living master craftsmen in Holland. He asked me once to calculate how many bricks he would need to make a semi-circular arch above a doorway, taking into account the amount of cement between the bricks and that the center brick had to be exactly in the middle. I worked on that problem for nearly an hour before I found the answer. He did it in less than a minute. "You studied all that arithmetic and you can't even figure out a simple problem," he joked. I asked him how he did it, but he refused to tell me. "When you become a bricklayer I'll tell you."

"With the depression and the war there hasn't been much work for a long time and because dad is his own boss, he isn't eligible for unemployment benefits."

Bets shook her head. "That must be tough."

"Mother sews for the ladies in the big houses and my sister works in a factory. Dad takes odd jobs, like making a fireplace or a garden wall here and there. My younger brother is still in school and, except during holidays, I study, because no matter what, I had to become a doctor. 'You have the brains, use them,' Dad always says. So now you know it all."

The sisters looked at me intently while I was talking. Their eyes never moved away from my direction. Unlike her younger sister, Bets was small and slightly built. Everything about her was small, including her hands and feet. Her eyes were softer than those of her sister were and it was much more evident that she was blind. The right eye was glazed and not centered. She wore her long gray hair in a bun on the back of her head. Both sisters wore old-fashioned long dresses, but they were stylish and not at all conservative in color. Bets wore the same golden necklace as Ann.

It had become dark outside and it was time to go home.

"Oh, I nearly forgot. I'll take the job," I said.

Ann laughed. "Fine. See you tomorrow." She let me out.

27

2

Driving Ann

At seven o'clock on the morning of September 21, 1942, I reported for work to give Ann a ride to the Institute. It took about forty-five minutes. After dropping her off, I rushed back to Rembrandt Avenue, parked the tandem in the garage, raced on my own bike to the small adjunct railroad station at Lapers Veld, and hopped on the train for the twenty minutes ride to Utrecht, where the medical school was located. Lectures usually lasted until four o'clock, after which I hurried back to the railroad station in Utrecht. The train to Hilversum left at four-thirty and in order to catch it, I ran all the way. Sometimes, if I was lucky, I jumped on a passing trolley car and got off before the conductor came by to collect the fee, which I didn't have. Back in Hilversum, I rode as fast as I could to Rembrandt Avenue and then, once again changing my bike for the tandem, went to the Institute, where Ann was always playing something on the piano while waiting for me. I sneaked in and listened at the door without making a sound. At the end of the piece she tilted her head, held it still like a pointer stalking a pheasant, listened, and said, "Are you there?" Or "You are here, aren't you?"

Riding that bike with Ann was fun. She told stories of her youth, of the numerous eye examinations by specialists, all of which ended in disappointments. There were stories about the Institutes she and Bets had been in, about her family, all the time joking and laughing in spurts as she and Bets did, their heads going up and to the side. Ann's head tilted to the right, Bets' to the left. We rode through the snow and blistering cold northwest winds of winter, the heat of summer and the rain of all seasons. She never complained and kept an upbeat mood at all times. From her, I learned about music, which was entirely new to me, and from me, she learned about the world around her and she asked many questions.

"What kind of truck was that?" she said when a German army truck thundered by.

"How do you dissect a frog?"

"Are they ours?" she asked when we heard planes high overhead.

"Yes they are. Did you know that those planes leave white lines in the sky?"

"No, how come?"

"I don't know exactly how, but when they fly really high the exhausts from their engines leave white vapor lines. Right now the sky is full of them. It's beautiful."

Behind me Ann didn't say much for a while. Maybe I shouldn't have said it, the beauty part. One ride that summer of 1942, I told her how we had made the German higher-ups in The Hague truly angry. During school vacation, I had taken a temporary job as an assistant administrator for a traveling fair. The fair consisted of the usual merry-go-rounds, electric car rides, Ferris wheels, games of chance, a fat lady, motor bikes racing in a large steel cage, two women doing things underwater, a calf with two heads, all sorts of other entertainment and many refreshment booths. Two brothers organized the fair and they hired a temporary assistant in every town. In our town, I became that assistant. I worked on the books in the back of a caravan that doubled as an office and conference room. In my spare time, I helped the brothers out by collecting money on one of two Flying Wheels they owned. These consisted of a large disc, about sixty feet in diameter, tilted at a thirty-degree angle. The seats were arranged at

29

the periphery so that two persons could sit side by side. A foot-wide platform on the outside helped the passengers getting in and out of their seats. We used it to stand on while collecting the fee and always jumped off at the last moment.

Every fee collector cheated by palming the change, and I was no exception. I did it with German soldiers, especially those with a Dutch 'traitor whore' at their side. If occasionally one of them protested that I hadn't given him back the correct amount, I simply jumped off the now fast moving ride. There was no way he could get off until the wheel came to a complete stop and by that time I had long disappeared in the crowd.

After fourteen days in our town, the fair was supposed to close on Sunday and travel the next day to Utrecht. However, on Saturday an order came down from the German occupation headquarters in The Hague that the fair could no longer use the railroad to transport its heavy wagons. The two brothers and other stand owners were furious. They crowded in the caravan and raised a racket. Finally, the older of the two brothers quieted them down.

"Listen up. We'll try to straighten it out. Just go about your business and we'll let you know how it turns out. Now get the hell out of here." He turned to me.

"Barth, you speak German don't you? Get on the phone and see what you can do. I don't give a damn how you do it, but we have to get that order reversed."

I called everywhere — cajoled, pleaded, threatened and finally got through to the office of Dr. Seyss-Inquart, the reviled German High Commissioner for Holland. He had a stiff leg as a result of a fall while walking in the Alps and moved around with a cane. We lost no time in calling him "6 ¼," because in Dutch, Seyss-Inquart and "6 ¼" sound almost the same—*zes en een kwart*. Another nickname was "hinkelepink," which is a derisive name for someone with a limp. Seyss-Inquart was an Austrian, whose treachery in 1938 had forced the resignation of Austrian Chancellor Schuschnigg. Soon thereafter he had maneuvered the so-called 'Anschluss' to unite his home country with Germany. In May of 1940, Hitler appointed him as High Commissioner of Holland. When Seyss-Inquart heard the news of the appointment, he enthusiastically phoned his wife. "Trude, the Führer wants me to plant tulip bulbs," but Gertrude Maschka, his wife since 1916, was less enthralled with the idea of living in a country where most people were hostile. In his inaugural address on May 29, he said, "I did not come to take away your freedom," and than proceeded to do just that.

An adjutant answered the phone.

"What's the meaning of the order that the fair can no longer use railroad flat beds to move from city to city?"

I raised my eighteen-year-old voice as loud as I could. When taking the offensive against the Germans, it was best to speak in a loud voice, otherwise they walked all over you.

"Don't you know that we provide the entertainment for your occupation troops?" I slipped the word 'occupation' in.

"Warten Sie mal," the adjutant snapped back.

I could almost see him come to attention. He needed to consult with the higher-ups about this, maybe even with Seyss-Inquart himself.

"Alles in Ordnung," he came back after a long wait. "Es war ein Missverständnis."

Some misunderstanding. In the future, we could use the trains again, but not the next day, when we were supposed to move to Utrecht. That he couldn't arrange on such short notice. However, we were nevertheless expected to start the fair in Utrecht on Tuesday. This meant that we had to haul the heavy wagons over the road. From all over town, we collected strong Belgian and Dutch draft horses and on that hot Sunday afternoon in August, we pulled the heavy wagons with their wide, steel-rimmed wheels over the twelve-mile-long asphalt road between Hilversum and Utrecht. By late that evening, when the last wagons had arrived, there

31

wasn't much left of the road surface. The heavy wheels had sunk deep into the sun-warmed asphalt and the horses had clawed the soft surface to pieces with their hooves. Dutch repair crews were in no particular hurry to fix the road and traffic between Hilversum and Utrecht stood at a standstill for days. The Germans had good reason to be angry, but they had brought it on themselves and there wasn't much they could do about it.

When I finished the story, Ann laughed and laughed. She couldn't stop laughing, couldn't pedal any longer and we had to get off by the side of the road. She doubled over; tears of laughter rolled down her cheeks. And that made me laugh too. Passersby threw curious eyes at the strange couple, laughing their heads off. Naturally, I had to repeat the whole story for Bets when we came home. She had one question.

"What do you mean by palming money?"

The best way to explain something like that to the ladies was by demonstration.

"Feel my hand. How many coins do I have and what kind?"

She carefully felt the palm of my hand with her soft fingers.

"Five. A quarter, a dime, a five cent piece and two pennies."

"Good. Now hold up your right hand and I'll give you the coins."

She examined the coins in her hand and laughed.

"You kept the quarter."

"Right. Now you do it. Hold up your hand again."

She held out her left hand and I put the five coins on it.

"Give me your other hand. Do you feel where I am holding my hand?"

"Yes, below my left hand."

"I want you to slide your left thumb over a coin like that and then turn your hand over so that the other coins will fall in my hand." She did and was delighted.

32

*Ann, Bets and Riek Frank in a 1909 photo when they opened
their music school.*

"You, Bets Frank, have been found guilty of palming the change. Now you teach Ann how you did it."

I left the sisters, who were already eagerly practicing the age-old art of petty thievery. On the way home, I remembered Ann doubling over with laughter. She had never seen anybody laugh like that. Doubling over must be a natural reaction of the human body, I thought. From that day on, I usually spent a little time with them after bringing Ann home. The sisters loved to hear the many jokes the war brought on, especially those that mocked the Germans.

"You have heard the Germans sing while marching through town, haven't you?"

"Sure, and they sing rather well," Ann said.

" Well, do you know what we do when they finish their favorite song, 'Gehen wir fahren gegen Engeland' (We are sailing against England)?"

"No, I don't know," Bets said.

"We add 'Plomp, plomp' the sound of them falling in the sea. Our other favorite addition is 'Eat cork and you may stay afloat.' "

Bets and Ann had never heard that. Soon after the American troops landed in North Africa, a new joke began circulating in Holland. Like so many of these, it was in German. It translated to "Me and my brother Heinrich, together with two other strong German soldiers, have killed one weak American."

Another time I told them how on a Sunday afternoon my brother and I were forced to teach two Waffen SS officers the art of sailing. They came marching up the dock of the Boomhoek, where our boat was moored, and ordered us to teach them. There they stood, like two marionettes, in their Sunday-best uniforms, all spit and polish, officer caps with the dreaded SS skull insignia jauntily askew on their heads. We were operating a small, one-boat sailing school at the time and tried to ignore them.

"Hey you!" the senior officer shouted.

"Me?"

"Jawohl. Teach us how to sail."

There was no way we could refuse. They were the masters in Holland.

"Take your boots off before you come aboard," I said.

"Nein."

"Ja."

"Niemals."

"Perhaps they have holes in their socks," Jaap snickered.

"What did you say?" the officer shouted.

"Nothing."

It was obvious that they weren't going to take any orders from two young Dutchmen. Without further ado, they clomped aboard with their hobnailed boots and immediately ruined the beautiful mahogany deck, the pride and joy of every sailor. It made us mad as hell and we decided to teach them a lesson about boats that they wouldn't easily forget. I told the ranking officer to kneel down on the side of our boat and to hold on to the one moored next to us, supposedly to avoid bumping into it as we left the dock. He was in a fine mood and laughed at his friend as he went down on his knees and leaned over to grab the other boat, not knowing that he would be the victim of an old sailor's trick. On the dock, people began to gather in expectation of what they knew was coming next. The boats were only fastened at the bow and slowly but surely they began to drift apart. He held on while the gap between the boats became wider and wider, and soon it was too late. He was forced to lean forward further and further until he was almost completely stretched out. He scowled at his now laughing fellow officer and ordered him to give a hand, but that only made matters worse. The boats continued to drift apart and soon they both fell in the water. The people on the dock howled with laughter. Cursing and screaming, the soldiers swam to the dock, while ordering us to stay put. Of course, we just sailed away.

Bets and Ann loved the story and the questions came in a flurry, mostly from Bets. It seemed so simple. Two arrogant German officers in their best Sunday uniforms ordering us around, refusing to take their boots off, ending up standing on the dock like two drowned cats. The scene was so easy to visualize, but how could they visualize when their eyes had never seen the light of day? They had simple questions.

"Why did they have to take their boots off?"

"Did they have a revolver?"

"Could they shoot you?"

Most of all they were puzzled as to why the soldiers had fallen in the water. No matter how carefully I explained the drifting apart of the two boats, it remained incomprehensible to them. Once again I resorted to a demonstration for which they eagerly volunteered. I put the piano stool in the middle of the room and maneuvered the sisters to one side of it.

"All right, ladies. Down you go, on your knees."

They laughed, pulled their long skirts up, and kneeled side by side.

"Now lean forward and get a hold of the piano stool. I am going to pull the stool away and you must keep your hands on the stool. You are not allowed to crawl forward on your knees, no matter what happens. Ready?"

"Yes," they both said.

They too stretched out further and further as I pulled the stool away from them and in the end they fell flat on the floor, still laughing. Now they understood that a boat in water doesn't give a firm handhold. It was all new to them and, as time went by, I learned that in order to satisfy their never-ending curiosity I had to describe scenes in much greater detail. They had never before heard those kinds of stories and it opened a whole new world for them, with me as their lifeline.

"That was fun," Bets said.

"Yes it was," Ann agreed. "I'm beginning to understand much better how this occupation affects so many parts of our life, even the little ones."

In a way it was amazing how little the sisters really knew. They didn't know that on April 29, 1942, the Nazis had ordered all Jews to wear the Star of David, with the word 'Jew' in the center, on their left chest. They borrowed the idea from Pope Innocent III, who in 1205 had issued a doctrine that Jews were doomed to perpetual servitude as Christ-killers. Ten years later, that same Holy Father decreed that Jews had to wear on their left chest a badge made of yellow felt. Convicted heretics and prostitutes were ordered to wear the same badge. Seven centuries later, the Nazis copied the decree, even to the point that the Star of David was made of yellow felt. All this was new to the sisters, who were intensely interested in anything historical.

"Do you know what happened to our town hall?" I asked one day.

"No," Bets said. She lifted her head, a bit puzzled. "I don't know where that is."

"It's about half a mile from here."

"Is it a nice building?" Ann said.

"It's beautiful. Dudok van Heel, who is a world famous architect, designed it and people from all over come to see it. It's made of a thin, light yellow brick. It has a high tower and there are fountains in front and back."

I stopped there, because from their blank faces it was clear that my description of the building made no impression on them.

"We have trouble imagining something that large without having been in it," Ann said. "It is difficult with something bigger than a house."

"I think I understand. Anyway, did you know that our

town hall now houses the headquarters of General Friedrich Christiansen, the commander of the Wehrmacht in Holland?"

"No. When did that happen?" Ann asked rather indifferently.

"Well, the order for evacuation went out on April 1, 1942, and the municipal services were given only six days to clear out."

"Six days. Was that enough time? How many people had to move? Where did they go."

"I don't know how many persons work there, but it is a big building. I understand that the Revenue Service went to the Saint Aloysius School, the Administration is now in the Catholic Labor Union building, and Public Works are next to the railroad station. We must now collect our food stamps in the loge of the freemasons. And you know what? You now have to get married in Grand Hotel Gooiland."

Bets laughed. "At least they don't have to go far for the party afterwards."

"You should see the building now. The tower is completely camouflaged and there are anti-aircraft guns on the roof. Last week, the entire area around the town hall was blocked off because Seyss-Inquart and SS General Rauter came for a meeting."

"They should bomb the place while they are in it," Bets said. "Then we get rid of them in one hit."

3

Sunday Afternoon Teas

A month after I began driving Ann, the sisters invited me for Sunday tea. It was an eye opener. They took great pride in making the tea themselves and knew exactly where everything was in the kitchen. With one hand, Ann found a container on a shelf. She brought her other hand to it, lifted the container up with two hands, and placed it carefully on the kitchen table. Bets filled the kettle with water. With her left hand, she felt for the edge of the burners of the gas range and with the other hand she centered the kettle on the burner. She turned on the gas and with a special device produced the sparks to light the gas. The big surprise came when Ann put real tealeaves in the pot.

"Where on earth did you get real tea?" I said. The import of tea from Java had stopped on the first day of the war and I hadn't tasted real tea in two years.

"We remembered how long the 1914 to 18 war lasted, so we bought a large supply immediately after the Germans came. We use it for special occasions and today is special," Bets said, her chin up and her lips in a fine smile. "We love tea."

When the kettle whistled, she carefully poured the boiling water into the pot and stopped pouring just in time so that the water didn't spill over. It was yet another wonderment.

39

35 Rembrandt Avenue

"How do you know when to stop pouring?" I said.

"By the change in sound when the water comes near the top," she replied and put the pot in a tea cozy. We proceeded to the living room, with Ann carrying the cups and saucers on a tray and Bets the tea cozy. I followed them, empty handed. Ann did the honors. She spooned sugar from the bowl and with one finger delicately felt to make sure that there was the right amount in the spoon. Using both hands, she maneuvered the spout of the teapot above a cup and poured. Many years of experience had taught her when to stop pouring. It took a little longer to pour the three cups, but she did it. She carefully picked one cup and saucer from the tray, turned in my direction and offered it to me. The smell of the real tea was delicious and I savored that first cup.

When we finished drinking, Ann said, "Bets and I have been talking about you and we both feel that we would like to know you better. But first we'll tell you something about us." She turned to her sister, "You want to start or shall I?"

"You go first," said Bets.

"We were born in Amsterdam. Our father used to sail on the big ships to the Indies, but after he met mother he took a job as cargo master. Mother . . . ."

"We are half Dutch, half Norwegian," Bets said.

"She had eight children," Ann continued as if Bets had not interrupted her. "Three boys, three blind girls and two normal girls. Our sister Riek, Bets and I were born blind."

"Actually we were lucky," Bets said. "In those days blind children of poor families usually ended up in the poorhouse weaving baskets."

"That's right, we went to the blind institute and fortunately all three of us were musically talented. Riek has a beautiful voice and she now sings professionally. She performed several times with the Concert Gebouw Orchestra under Willem Mengelberg and she toured with him."

"Who is Mengelberg?" I asked.

41

"Don't you know?" Bets was amazed at my ignorance.

"No. Never heard of him."

"He is a world famous conductor, like Paganini."

"Yes, now I remember his name, but isn't he sympathetic to the Germans?"

"I wouldn't be surprised," said Ann. "Anyway, Riek sang with him before the war. I played for Queen Mother Emma, when she visited the Institute in eighteen ninety seven. And two years later, I played Chopin's Nocturne in E Sharp for her daughter, Wilhelmina, when she was our new Queen. She was only nineteen years old."

"And how old were you?" I asked.

"She was all of nine years," Bets laughed.

"I have been invited a few times for tea in the palace in Amsterdam and Queen Wilhelmina gave me that grand piano." She pointed in the direction of the black piano. "And I sang children's songs for Princess Juliana when she was young."

Now it was Bets' turn.

"When I was twelve we were moved to the new Institute for the Blind in Amsterdam. We studied music, five languages and even calculus. The headmistress of that Institute was sort of a tight wad and quite often we didn't get enough to eat. Then Riek sneaked into the kitchen at night and brought us bread. Sunday was the best day, because in the afternoon we had tea with a biscuit. Twice a month and never on weekdays."

"Did they ever let you outside?"

"Oh yes. Once a day we were aired," Bets said, laughing in the same short bursts, as did her sister. But unlike Ann, she tilted her head up and to the left. "There was a garden behind the Institute. Actually there were two large squares of grass with paths around them, one square for the boys and the other for the girls. The paths were lined with a steel cable about a foot from the ground and we were supposed to feel our way around with a cane, but we all knew exactly how many steps each side took and so we just ran. We also jumped rope."

"We were always thirsty. The mistress limited our drinks because she didn't want any 'accidents' as she called it," said Ann. "When I was eighteen, I applied for the teacher's diploma for the piano, for elementary level and for advanced teaching. The Board of National Examiners refused to let me sit for the exam. "A blind person cannot play the piano, let alone teach it," they decided. "Especially not a woman." The headmistress was furious and she pushed through that I could take the examination. But instead of the usual three examiners, there were at least twenty. They were all curious to hear what a blind woman could do on the piano. And then I went for a year to Berlin to study at the famous Musik Hochschule," she added dryly as if that was nothing."

"And you just took the train and left, didn't you?" I said.

"Well, a teacher from the Institute escorted me."

"When Ann came back in 1909, we opened a music school in Amsterdam at number One Anna Vondel Street," said Bets. "Riek gives singing lessons, Ann and I teach the piano and Ann also acts as our business manager."

"How old were you when you opened that school?" I asked.

"I was twenty-three, Riek was twenty-one and Ann nineteen."

"Amazing. And where did the money come from? You couldn't just go to a bank and ask for it."

"We really don't know," said Bets. "I never asked. But some benefactor paid for our entire education, paid for Ann to stay in Berlin and then made an arrangement with a bank."

"Did you ever think who that may have been?"

"We were never told," said Bets.

"Well, I beginning to have a sneaky feeling that it may have been the Queen."

43

"Could be," Ann said noncommittal and she continued, "Actually we did pretty well with the school. But Riek married in 1925 and so Bets and I opened this school in Hilversum. And here we are."

"Now you know more about us than we do," Bets laughed. "Shall we have another cup?"

While Ann poured, I asked if their necklaces had a special meaning.

"It is the symbol of our religion," she said. "It was founded by our Leader in 1928 while he was in a German prison. He was condemned for political reasons and during that time he wrote a book about a new religious belief that centered on the Holy Grail. According to our Leader, life on earth is only a way station for the continual travel of the soul up or down a ladder. The soul can temporarily house in a tree and if it is a good tree it can after death come back to earth in a higher form of life, maybe as a horse or a human. If it didn't live a good life, it will be sent back a few steps. Ultimately the soul can reach the Holy Grail, Heaven. The symbol of our religion is what you see in our necklace."

"Hitler wrote 'Mein Kampf' while he was in prison. You think it may be a coincidence that your Leader did the same? Write a book I mean?"

"Maybe." She had no further comment.

Now I understood what Bets had meant when she made that comment about Karel, the boy in the hospital, going up the ladder. They showed me several photographs of the cult headquarters, which was located in the Austrian Alps. The Leader, a tall lean man, wore a white, ankle-length gown adorned with a golden stole and a large golden symbol in the middle of his chest. His wife, who was in charge of the women, also wore a stole and a symbol, but hers were silver. Bets and Ann, like the other followers in the photographs, wore plain white gowns. A thought occurred to me about the photos.

"These photographs. You can't see them, so why do you have them?"

What I thought was an innocent question provoked an immediate change in both women. They became dead serious.

"We are blind, but that doesn't mean that we can't be the same as other people."

Ann's face and voice were stern. "We have photos just like everybody else. Not for us to look at but we can show them and it helps with conversation. You must never consider us as invalids, as helpless, as different. Otherwise, we can't be friends."

"We are normal people," Bets said quietly.

I felt chastised. The silence was palpable. Bets cleared her throat.

"We do not have churches," she said. "We meet in each others house once a month. Now, that's enough talk about us. Why don't you tell us something about the war? We only know what we hear over the radio and from what a pupil says now and then, but we really don't know much about it."

"Well, I better first give you some of the background. To begin with, do you know what a fascist is, what fascism stands for."

"The German political party?" Ann tried.

"Not really. The word 'fascist' comes from 'fascis', the Latin word for 'bundle'. It was a bundle of rods, bound around the handle of an ax, and during the reign of the Roman emperors, it was carried by the police as a symbol of the power of the state. Mussolini, that pompous dictator of Italy, likens himself as an emperor and in 1922 he became the first fascist. He said that fascism is the dictatorship of the state over all classes. A few years later Hitler also liked the word, but he gave a it a different meaning. He said that the state is a living organism in which the individuals are only cells in the service of the state. Hitler and Mussolini both changed their

45

countries into totalitarian states, in which the men and women have nothing to say and are completely controlled by huge secret police forces. And they had followers in other countries as well. In 1933, a Norwegian by the name of Vidkun Quisling founded the Nasjonal Samling (National Union Party). Soon afterwards he was forced to resign as Minister of Defense of Norway. Three days before the German army invaded his country, he returned from Berlin, where he had assisted the Germans in finalizing the plans for invading his country. His years as Minister of Defense had come in handy in this betrayal and his name became synonymous with the foulest form of perfidy. Here in Holland, Anton Mussert, who was a senior engineer of the Department of Roads and Water, formed the National Socialist Party, the NSB, on December 14, 1931, eighteen months before Hitler took power in Germany. Mussert knew every detail of Holland's main line of defense against a possible German invasion, namely the flooding of the lowlands. He told the Germans that they would have a difficult time overcoming that obstacle. And when in May 1940, the German army invaded our country, the water indeed stopped their heavy tanks cold. That's when they resorted to the bombing of Rotterdam, the first open city to be bombed in this war. They then threatened that unless the Dutch army surrendered, they would bomb Utrecht next and other cities thereafter.

"No wonder our government gave in," said Bets.

The Dutch radio stations and newspapers were completely under German control and fed us only the highly biased news that the Nazi propaganda machine saw fit for consumption for the people in the occupied countries. Listening to the BBC was prohibited and when someone was caught doing it, he was severely punished and usually ended up in a slave labor camp. The Germans frequently drove around in a truck with an antenna on top. With it they could locate a radio that was tuned to the BBC. Like so many other people, we at home also listened to Radio Orange. The BBC generously allotted some time to each occupied country, so that its representatives living in London could send news from the free world in their native tongue to their country. Radio Orange also used that time to transmit coded messages to the Dutch underground forces.

"The cow is chasing the dog."

"The coffee is poured."

"Aunt Mary had a baby girl."

The messages were always repeated to make sure that they had been heard and clearly understood. Everybody knew that these short sentences, which made little sense, were meant as messages for members of the underground. When it was time for Radio Orange to come over the air waves, young boys and girls stood at the corners of the streets on the lookout for the German truck and signaled when they saw one approaching. From Radio Orange, from discussions with fellow students, from what we saw happening outside, and even from our newspapers, which were all controlled by the Nazis, I gained a fairly good picture of the war.

The fact that the Germans ordered us to turn in all objects made of copper, brass and tin showed that they were running short in vital materials for their war machine. Their call for blankets and woolen underwear meant that they had been ill prepared for the severe Russian winters. The young and vigorous soldiers of the occupation force were more and more replaced by middle-aged men in ill-fitting uniforms. No longer were the radio stations and newspapers glorifying the heroic submarine commanders, from which we deducted that the Allies had found better ways to protect the convoys.

The newspaper accounts of the war were most informative. The Germans, who knew that they couldn't hide everything, gave the news with their best slant. All we did was read between the lines. In the *Nationale Dagblad* issue of

47

Tuesday, February 9, 1943, I noticed four hidden indications of the turnaround that was taking place.

"A 5,000-ton ship that had lost contact with its convoy was sunk by a German submarine." The article did not mention a word about a concentrated attack on the convoy and a year ago a 5,000-ton ship was hardly worth mentioning.

"The Bolsheviks continued their ferocious attacks yesterday, supported by strong armored forces." Key words such as "continued" and "strong" were indications that the German army was in trouble on the Russian front.

"Allied airplanes dropped a few bombs in West Germany last night and damaged a few buildings." West Germany is a big territory, so we concluded that there must have been many planes.

"Dutch volunteers for the Waffen SS who object to serving outside the Netherlands, are now permitted to serve in a special guard battalion." Can you imagine? A member of the Waffen SS objecting? The Germans really must be short in manpower.

One of our biggest morale boosters was the Dutch underground press. Bernard IJzerdraat, a prophetic name meaning 'barbed wire,' created the first paper. He used to live in the Achterhoek, close to the German border, but, when on September 1, 1939, the Germans attacked Poland, he was convinced that sooner or later they would also cross the border of Holland as part of Hitler's expansion policy. When that happened, he wanted to fight them as long as possible. He moved his family to Schiedam in the Western part of Holland. On May 15, 1940, the day that our country capitulated after the infamous bombing of Rotterdam in which more than 30,000 people lost their lives, IJzerdraat wrote his first *Geuzen newsletter*. He took the name from a band of Dutchmen called 'Water Geuzen,' who in 1573 liberated Den Briel, the first Dutch town freed from the Spanish troops, who, led by the notorious Duke of Alva, had occupied Holland in 1568. That war lasted eighty years before Holland was free.

On May 18, IJzerdraat wrote his second letter, requesting that anyone who received it should make two copies and distribute them as one would a chain letter. In the letters, which were handwritten, he had purposefully made a few errors and distorted his writing. He advised others to do the same. I, too, distributed my two copies. IJzerdraat predicted exactly what would happen after the Germans occupied Holland. "Food, clothing, and shoe wear will be taken away. Soon food ration coupons will be issued and eventually even these will be of little value." He predicted that young men would be forced to work in Germany and that Holland would soon have a new Alva. He urged us to be brave and keep hope and trust. "Our land will never be a part of Germany. Dutchmen, do your Geuzen duty. Make two copies of this letter in distorted handwriting and give them to trusted friends. Let this be an uninterrupted chain action." To confuse the Germans, IJzerdraat mentioned that his letter came from Amsterdam, whereas in reality it was produced in Schiedam. He urged the people to remain calm.

IJzerdraat organized a group of underground fighters named 'Geuzen.' They were betrayed and on March 13, 1941, eighteen fighters, including IJzerdraat, were executed in he dunes of Holland. Many others died in Buchenwald, a notorious concentration camp. Jan Compert wrote the famous poem 'The Eighteen Dead' while in the camp. He too was executed.

Hilversum too had its illegal newspapers. *The Gooise Courier* was published by Hans Bantzinger and the brothers De Greef in a bedroom of a house that been declared as uninhabitable a few years before. Their paper was typewritten and they used three stencil machines to make copies. *Our Resistance* and *The Herald* were two papers distributed by a group of students from my high school. The group called itself 'De Strijders' or 'The Fighters.' These papers had a

49

special appeal for me, because they contained several carica-
tures by Rob Korpershoek, who graduated the same year I
did. He had always been good at drawing. His signature –
'm'— became famous and soon his drawings appeared in many
illegal newspapers. Annie Hoogstraten, no relation, and Mieke
Adama of our school were very much involved in the distribution of these papers. All this was happening during the first
year of occupation, when the Germans were still rather lax in
enforcing their law. However, after January 1941, their reign
of terror increased in intensity and everybody became more
careful.

Hilversum was the center of all radio stations in Holland
and when it became necessary to transmit illegal messages
to England, our town was a logical site. The restaurant Hof
of Holland was a favorite of the high-ranking officers of the
Wehrmacht. They never discovered that in one of the rooms
the Dutch had installed one of the strongest transmitters, which
was used throughout the war.

Since the Dutch newspapers only gave a biased view of
the war, the leaders of the Dutch underground, realizing the
importance of maintaining the morale of the citizenry, soon
began to add news from the Allied side of the war in the
illegal press. And they gave traitors a new name, Quislings.

Bets excused herself to go to the bathroom. I was quiet
and Ann sensed that something was wrong.

"I shouldn't have said that about us not being friends,"
she said.

She got up, felt for my shoulders and gave me an almost
shy hug, which made me feel better.

"So Mussert is just as bad as Quisling," Bets said when
she returned.

"That's right, and I think that the only reason why the
Dutch call them Quislings is because it sounds worse than
Musserts."

Two prominent members of the National Socialist Party,

the NSB, played important roles in the events of late 1942 and early 1943 that affected the lives of every student. First, on December 9, 1942, the new Secretary-General of Education, Professor J. van Dam, announced that fifty percent of the students would have to go to Germany as part of the 'Arbeitseinsatz,' their word for a slave labor pool. The Student Unions immediately called for a student strike, which effectively closed the universities, and suddenly I had all the time in the world to drive Ann.

The second NSB member, retired Lt. General Hendrik Alexander Seyffardt, was the organizer of the Dutch volunteer force that fought alongside the Germans on the Eastern Front in Russia. In the early 1930s, Seyffardt had been Chief of the Dutch military staff and Chairman of the Council of Defense. In 1937, he became a member of the NSB, but resigned six months later.

"I probably can be more useful to the Party if I am no longer known as a member," he announced.

Useful for what? His appointment on February 4, 1943, as Deputy Commander of the Dutch Legion proved to be fatal for him. CS-6, one of the most aggressive underground cells, so named because the two leaders lived on Corelli Street 6 in Amsterdam, decided to act. Two of its members, a psychiatrist, Dr. Gerard Kastein, who was a Communist, and a 23 year-old Catholic student, Jan Verleun, rang the door bell of Seyffardt's house in The Hague. He opened the door himself.

"Are you General Seyffardt?"

"Yes. What do you want?"

Jan Verleun answered by putting two bullets in the abdomen of the 70 year-old Seyffardt. It was the first time that the Dutch underground used this form of liquidation. Seyffardt lived for another day and shortly before his death blamed the students for the attack. He asked that no hostages be executed as a result of his assassination, but that same day,

51

another Austrian, head of the Nazi Police, SS General Hanns Albin Rauter, announced that fifty hostages would be shot. The SS and Gestapo always had a reserve of hostages available for such purpose. Especially in the larger towns, they needed only the slightest excuse to round up fifty or more men and hold them prisoners for undetermined lengths of time, usually three to six months. On large bulletins, which were tacked on trees and buildings all over town, they announced that they would execute a number of hostages in retaliation for any 'murder' of a German soldier or Dutch member of the NSB. The number shot was determined by the relative importance of the victim. A mere Dutch Nazi might be worth five hostages, a German soldier twenty or more, depending on his rank. They set the price. General Seyffardt was worth fifty lives.

Rauter also led his troops in a series of raids on the universities of Amsterdam, Utrecht, Delft, and Wageningen. On March 13, Seys-Inquart, the German High Commissioner, demanded that all Dutch students annually sign a declaration of loyalty to the occupation forces. In this document the student promised to refrain from all resistance to the occupation force, "which had so courageously liberated Holland at the request of the NSB." Those who refused to sign were threatened with severe punishment. All students were also automatically registered for the Dutch Labor Force, a phony vehicle used by the Germans to recruit extra manpower for work on their defense installations in Holland. No signature was needed for that registration. My enlistment number was 43-1-IV-12, and I could be called to serve any time in 1943.

From that time on, Rauter began terrorizing the Dutch like never before. Men of all ages were rounded up for even the slightest provocation and untold numbers were executed or transferred to concentration camps. It became so bad that the leaders of the underground decided to kill Rauter no matter what the costs would be. This was an extremely painful decision, because the SS would undoubtedly retaliate furiously for the slaying of their leader. Volunteers ambushed Rauter's car near the town of Putten and after a short firefight, summarily executed him. The next day, the SS herded all men ages 18 to 50 into the town square. Seventy-one were excused on the spot and the rest, 589, were deported to their most notorious concentration camp, where 552 lost their lives. The citizens of Putten paid a terrible price for the death of that monster.

The loyalty declaration caused a split amongst the students. Even though they were anti-German, some students signed because they wanted to continue their study and didn't think that their signature was meaningful. A few signed because they were scared. The majority refused to sign any German order. My parents agreed with my decision not to sign. That evening, after I drove Ann home, I told the sisters what had happened. They listened without interrupting and in the end were glad that I hadn't signed. But, they had one important question.

"Since you didn't sign that declaration, what'll happen to you?"

"I don't know. Maybe one day they'll put me in a labor unit. But one thing is sure, I'll never go to Germany. I'll go underground instead."

"Where? How?" Ann said.

"I don't know yet. Probably in Loosdrecht. I know the lakes and marshes quite well and we have many friends there."

Nothing happened for a while. I continued to drive Ann to the institute and after a few weeks, the universities opened their doors again. Other Sunday tea sessions followed and with their never satisfied curiosity the sisters wanted to learn all about me.

53

4

Gijs and Ali

"We would like you to tell us something about your family," Ann said the next Sunday when we sat around sipping tea. I noticed that when they asked a question, they tilted their heads ever so slightly up and to the side, Ann to the right and Bets to the left. The movement seemed to be part of the asking.

"Well, I was born on the thirteenth of May 1924, in Loosdrecht on the dairy farm of Daan Heineke."

"Like Heineken beer!" Bets recognized a familiar name.

"Right. Our parent's names are Gijs and Ali. There was a serious housing shortage in Holland when they married in 1920, and they were lucky to find two rooms with their friend Daan, next to the stable. The minister of the old church, Dr. Vellemga, baptized me Bartholomeus after mother's father and she told me years later that Vellemga hoped that I would follow in the footsteps of the apostle, but as you can see that did not happen. Have you been in Loosdrecht?"

"No we haven't," Ann said.

"Loosdrecht is a small town, only three miles from here. It actually consists of two parts—Old and New Loosdrecht— with the town hall in between. I think it has only one street, but it is a long street, about four miles long. It curves around the five man-made lakes."

"What do you mean by man-made?" asked Bets.

"It means that they are not natural lakes. Many centuries

ago, the entire area consisted of peat, which was the most precious form of fuel at the time and the only way of heating houses and castles. The farmers harvested the peat and sold it to the surrounding towns, but mainly to Amsterdam and Utrecht. After many years they had harvested the upper layers of peat and water began to seep through. During the summer months, they dredge the bog deeper and deeper and let it dry the land. In the fall, when all the water had seeped out, they cut it to make peat bricks. And that's how the lakes were made."

"I thought they were called 'plassen'," said Ann.

"That's right. We simply call them the First, Second, Third, Fourth and Fifth Plas. The name Loosdrecht comes from the combination of two words; 'drecht' which means 'dredge' and 'loos' is 'drain', letting the water drain out after they dredged the bog. And that's how the name came about."

"Do you have any brothers and sisters?" asked Bets.

"Yes, two. My sister Coosie is a year older than I and my brother Jaap is four years younger. And all three of us have red hair."

"I like red," said Bets.

I nearly bit my lips not asking why she liked red.

"In 1930 my parents could finally rent a house in Hilversum, on Marconi Street. It was the last street before the heather began and close to the slaughterhouse. When the wind came from that direction, you could smell the mixture of cattle and blood. In the heather, about three hundred feet away, stood a small brick building. That's where they burned the carcasses of dead animals, but at least they waited until the wind was to the north. The thick, black smoke coming from the chimney of the building on the heather was a dead give-away. "They burned another one," Mother would say when Dad came home."

"It must have been a horrible smell," said Ann.

"At least they always waited until the wind came from

the South, away from us. But sometimes the wind direction changed while they were burning and then the whole house smelled. The dead animals attracted rats, and we had rats in our yards, in the sheds, all over the place. The wives complained bitterly and annoyed their husbands to the point that they finally decided to organize a rat hunt. They closed off all escape routes and then, armed with shovels, axes, and clubs, began chasing the rats from their hideouts, but not before putting the bottom of the pants in their socks to prevent a desperate rat from running up their pants and biting their testicles. At least that's what my Dad claimed to be the truth. We boys were put on top of the sheds to sight the rats.

"There goes one and there another one," we yelled at the top of our lungs and the men ran after them, whooping and hollering. A good haul was 20 to 30 rats, some as big as rabbits. After the hunt, we got a glass of lemonade and the men went to the nearest pub to celebrate their victory over the varmints. "We need to wash the dust from our throats," they said. They had a good time and after the first hunt, their wives never again needed to urge them on."

"I don't like rats," said Bets and she changed the subject. "Were you a good student?"

"I think so. I was the only one of my class to go to the HBS."

"What is that?" asked Ann.

"That stands for Higher Burger School. It is the only public high school in Hilversum and surrounding villages of het Gooi, maybe eighty thousand people in all. As you know 'burger ' is the same as 'citizen'. High school is still considered only for the privileged class and it is rare for a student from the working class to go to high school. My parents certainly could not afford the tuition, let alone the books. Sometimes they offered financial assistance for gifted students, and we were the so-called gratis students. Actually it is a school with very high standards and only one in five students manages to graduate without repeating a class."

"Why could your parents not pay the tuition?" Bets asked.

"Because Dad had not worked for several years. Mother made a green velvet jacket for me from curtains that were discarded at one of the houses where she worked. It had four pockets and a belt. She took me to the Salvation Army warehouse and picked out a pair of pants made of sturdy brown material. "They'll last," she said. Their owner must have been a fat man, but that was no problem. "I'll take them in," she said. She did not see, or pretended not to see, the yellowish discoloration just left of the fly. I hated those pants, always conscious of that spot, sure that other people would notice it. But I wore them and the green jacket for five years.

Dad rented a small plot of land from a farmer nearby. He grew his own vegetables and potatoes. No tomatoes—he hated tomatoes. He didn't like rice either. "That's chicken feed," he used to say. Mother cleaned, cut, and salted the vegetables and stored them in large earthen pots. Dad did odd jobs for the well-to-do folks—the gentry. They called him Gijs, he addressed them as 'mister' or 'ma'am.' Even at home he talked about them as such. He made a porch here, an open fireplace there, repaired a ceiling, and did most everything.

He was always on the lookout for things that might come in handy and one winter he spotted something on an old country road alongside a narrow canal, the 'Ten Farms Canal.' Only a few local farmers and an occasional man on a bicycle such as Dad used the road. The heavy, steel-rimmed wheels of the farm wagons and the clawing hooves of horses had exacted a toll on the old road and where the surface had broken down, Dad noticed that the foundation had been made of coke. From then on, in the early morning light, long before milking time, Dad and I began to collect the coke. We did it from the sides and in spots where other people wouldn't notice. The old road helped us through many cold winter months.

He also kept rabbits in cages in the backyard. Belgian giants, they were called. Always a male and female. After school hours, my brother Jaap and I collected grass for the rabbits, which was our contribution in fattening them up for Christmas. The male was put in a separate cage as soon as the female had a litter so that he wouldn't kill the newborns, which was bound to happen when he began to feel too confined in the now overcrowded cage. The day before Christmas, Dad took the male from his cage, held him upside down by the hind legs, and, with the handle of his knife hit him hard behind the ear. The struggling rabbit squealed something awful when Dad had missed the right spot one time and it took two or more hits before the rabbit was unconscious. Dad, an animal lover, felt bad about it for days. "Should have hit him better," he muttered. He cut an artery in the neck of the now limp animal and holding it by the ears and hind legs he let the blood run out. He then hung him by the hind legs from two nails, which he had hammered in the door of the shed for just that purpose and skinned it in two minutes flat. Starting just below the rib cage, he slit the abdomen open and let the intestines hang out, grayish-green, steaming in the cold winter air. In five minutes, he had that rabbit ready for the pot. Only some bloodstains remained in the snow. The two nails in the door wait for next year.

Mother really knew how to prepare it. In a cast iron pot over a gas flame, she brought the water, with the animal in it, to a boil, and then let it simmer for hours over the low flame of a kerosene stove. Soup was made from the heart, liver and kidneys. My sister Coos made a pair of gloves from the skin. The dog got the bones."

I suddenly became aware that the sisters hadn't said anything for quite a while. They remained silent until finally Ann said, "I thought that intestines were red."

"Actually they were thin and the green of the grass shines through. Our intestines are probably red."

"Your father sounds like a wonderful man," said Bets. "And your mother?"

"The best way to answer that is to ask whether you know what an 'Erfgooier' is."

"No," they said in unison.

"Well, her father was an 'Erfgooier'. This county where we live is called 'het Gooi'. In the thirteenth century, the farmers in 'het Gooi' organized themselves into a community to govern their land. Even the powerful Earls of Holland were forced to accept this unheard of expression of independence. They needed the peat. The farmers kept the land in perpetuity from father to oldest son and they called themselves 'Erfgooier'. The ground around the farm is called 'erf'. They were stubborn, stiff and headstrong and wellknown figures in this part of the country. My grandfather, Bart Knegt, was an 'Erfgooier' and mother has all the traits. She keeps her troubles inside her and that's probably the reason why she developed a stomach ulcer. I'll never forget the day when Dad came into our bedroom.

"I want you to be real quiet," he said. "Mother is very sick."

"What happened?" Jaap whispered.

"I'll tell you later. When it's time to get up, make no noise."

Mother had awakened in a pool of blood and would stay in bed for several months.

"Who did the household while she was sick?" Bets wanted to know.

"Coosie. She did everything and she was always cheerful. "We'll make it. You'll see," she kept saying.

"How old was she?" Ann asked.

"Ten,"

'What a brave girl. And what did you do?"

"Dad insisted that I study, but when I was eleven I began working with Dad during vacation time. He finally was the low bidder for the bricklaying and plasterwork for those new villas on the Kastanje Avenue. He needed new mortar and I helped Willem, his handyman, with the slaking of the limestone. We each had a pit to work with."

"What do you mean, pit? A pit is in fruit," said Bets.

"True, but to get lime you have to dig a hole in the ground, about six by ten feet and eight feet deep. That hole we called the pit. We put a foot of water in, threw in a layer of limestone rocks and immediately a chemical reaction started. The water began to boil and gave off thick clouds of foul smelling sulfuric acid. We raked the rocks until all the lime was out and then began a second layer."

"That sounds like unhealthy work," said Ann.

"It's worse than it sounds. Our lungs filled with the steam and we coughed all day. And the acid burned our eyes."

"You could have gone blind." Bets was concerned.

"Not me, but Willem's eyes were always tearing. He also coughed and spat a lot. Dad said that he had water on his heart, but I think that it came from his lungs. He died the next year."

"The poor man," Bets said and she left the room, while Ann poured more tea.

"What else did you do?" Bets asked when she came back.

"I helped Willem with the scaffolding and carried bricks and mortar to the workers. It was fine during dry days, but when it rained, the boards cut through the skin of my fingers in no time. "Willem, let the boy make the mortar for a while," Dad yelled down when he saw the blood."

"But your hands are soft," said Ann.

"That's because I haven't used them for a while."

"You didn't have much of a vacation, did you?" she said.

"Oh, it was only for two summers. But I didn't like it when my classmates drove by, going sailing or to play tennis, while I pushed a cart loaded with supplies. But they were too busy chatting and laughing and had no eyes for someone behind a pushcart. Now it is getting late and I better go home."

Ann brought me to the door.

"I want to give you a hug," she said and she did.

5

Going Underground

The sisters were fascinated with the stories about my family, but life took a serious turn early one day in May 1943. The German-controlled radio announced that all students who had not signed the loyalty declaration had to report immediately to the main railroad station of the town in which their university was located. From there they were to be transported to Germany and put to work in German factories and 'assist the German Reich in its final push towards a glorious victory over the enemies of democracy, freedom, and the Reich.' The announcer added that medical students would be put to work in hospitals. When I left home that morning to pick up Ann, a student raced by on his bike on his way to Utrecht.

"Barth, you can still sign," he yelled.

"No way," I yelled back.

The poor fellow fell into the trap the Germans had so cleverly set by spreading a rumor that students could still sign and thus avoid being deported. When he and others arrived ready to sign, they were immediately arrested and held for transportation to Germany. I told the sisters of the order, adding that this would be the last time for me to drive Ann.

"You're not going to sign, are you?" Bets asked. Something in her voice made me think that if my answer had been yes, she would have told me not to come back. But I had already made up my mind.

"I'm going underground."

"Where will you go?" Ann asked.

"I can't tell you that. It's much better for people not to know."

"Why?"

"Well, immediately after the Germans occupied Holland, the warning went out to be very careful with what you tell people. The saying, "What they don't know, they can't tell" has been used ever since. Not necessarily because people can't be trusted, but something may slip out inadvertently during a conversation and an enemy ear may pick it up. And the Germans stop at nothing when they want to find out something, not even torture."

What I said had a sobering effect on the sisters. Other than relatively small inconveniences, the occupation had not yet touched them at a personal level. Now it affected someone they felt close to and it made them think.

"We never realized that they could be that bad."

They stared straight ahead; the muscles of their jaws tightened. It was as if they were gathering strength, as if they were getting ready to face a new challenge.

I had given much thought about the consequences of my decision not to sign the loyalty declaration and had come to the conclusion that ultimately the Nazis would most likely force those who had refused to sign to go to Germany. That day was now. Without saying anything to my parents, I had discussed it with Dad's brother, Uncle Jaap. Some people said that he was a communist, but he really wasn't and I knew better. He was like so many other socialists, who admired what the communists had done for Russia before the war and the fierce battle they were giving the Germans now. His so-called communism was all talk. We all felt the plight of the Russian people.

Uncle Jaap had lived the carefree life of a bachelor, sailing, driving his large Harley Davidson, and going to motorbike races with his friends. But then his most recent girlfriend, Lies, got pregnant and he married at age forty. They lived with her

63

father in Kortenhoef, a small farming town much like Loosdrecht. It was one long road, with a canal and dairy farms bordering one side of the road and on the other side a thin strip of land that slowly went over into marches and lakes. Their house, which dated from seventeenth century, was built on that strip. They had four daughters and Jaap was as happy as a bee with his newly found life. He loved his father-in-law, a tall, good-looking townsman with a huge moustache, who served his church as sexton.

"Where is Pa?" he asked when he came home from work one day.

"Out in the field digging potatoes," Lies replied.

When the old man still hadn't come home an hour later, Jaap went looking for him. He found him in the field, with a basket between his knees, a cluster of potatoes in his hand and his head down on his chest. Jaap ran back home.

"Lies, Pa is sitting in the field stone dead." That said, he began to cry.

An intricate network of narrow waterways connected the marches and lakes of Kortenhoef with those of Loosdrecht. Only someone born in that area would know his way around. Unbeknown to all of us, even his brother, Uncle Jaap secretly hid a Jewish diamond merchant from Amsterdam, who, together with his wife and daughter, stayed throughout the war in a small room upstairs that Jaap had made for that purpose. The socialist helped rich people survive, without compensation, without God playing a role in his life. He, like so many others, just did it because it was the right thing to do.

Kortenhoef, like Loosdrecht, was an ideal place for someone to go into hiding. It was a small, tightly knit community of farmers. It was also a village known for its large laundries. Here the dirty linen of the well-to-do of Amsterdam, Hiversum, and Utrecht was washed. The small town industry provided work for untold numbers of people. The town was of little interest to the Germans. The long, single road made it almost impossible for them to stage an efficient raid. People could easily escape on either side of the road, into the marshes in a rowboat or into the fields across the canal. Unlike the larger towns, such as Hilversum, where the people were limited to food rations, the farms and the lakes of Kortenhoef also provided ample opportunity for extra food. It would be quite easy to build a hut on one of the numerous tiny islands in the marshes and stay hidden for a long time, while keeping in contact with Uncle Jaap. During the past year, I had made several trips to see him. He kept sheep on a few acres of land they owned across the street and Lies spun the wool on her spinning wheel. I wound the wool around my body under my clothes and smuggled it home on the way back to Hilversum. From it, Mother and sister Coos used it to make mittens and sweaters, which they sold to friends and neighbors.

"You're not going to work for those bastards, are you?" Uncle Jaap had said when I told him that I had not signed. "Tell you what. When the time comes that you have to go to Germany, come see me first."

It didn't work out that way. That evening, when I brought Ann back for the last time, Bets invited me to come underground in their house. Bets . . . the small woman with the quiet strength, the sister who at times could be so decisive that even Ann wouldn't dare disagree. Bets was the one who figured it all out while Ann was at the institute.

"Why don't you come and stay with us?" she said.

"Bets, you don't know what you're saying," I said, surprised. "It sounds so easy, but do you realize the danger you're putting yourself in?"

However, I didn't reject the offer outright. The idea of staying with these two fascinating women intrigued me. Their blindness, their world, everything about them was different from normal people. Bets didn't give me a chance to think much longer. She had made up her mind and introduced an argument that I hadn't thought about and couldn't dispute.

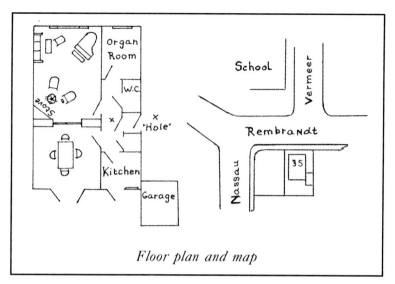

Floor plan and map

"Nobody will look for you in the house of two blind women."

Ann, who had been very quiet through all this, now also had something to add.

"We'll do as if you are also blind. We can teach you."

"It's easy; we have experience," said Bets. They both laughed, but it was clear that they had no idea of the real danger.

"What'll happen if the Germans ever stage a raid? They can throw you in prison if they find out about me."

"Even Germans aren't so dumb to do that to blind women," Ann replied.

They had made up their minds and refused to listen to any further arguments from me. Bets nailed it down.

"Think of the fun we'll have with a man in the house." She giggled in anticipation.

The next morning, I packed a suitcase and left my home en route to Germany, sent off with a kiss from my crying mother and a handshake from a somber father.

"You know how to take care of yourself," he said. "You'll be back."

The MULO school across the street

Sympathetic neighbors donated fruit and cookies for the long trip ahead. But instead of walking to the railroad station, I went in a roundabout way to the woods nearby. There I waited until it was dark before going to the house on Rembrandt Avenue. A few days later, I sent my parents a message that I was safe by the simplest and, amazingly, also the safest way open to us in those days—the mail. By not telling them of my plan to go underground in the first place, they had acted normally when I left—as concerned parents, who saw their son leave for an uncertain future in a country we all hated so much. And, more importantly, several neighbors had witnessed the departure, one of whom was a known member of the NSB, the Dutch Nazi Party. The house on number 35 Rembrandt Avenue had two fairly large rooms downstairs. The front room, the one with the grand piano, functioned as the music room and sitting room. The room in the back was used for dining and day-to-day living. It opened with French doors onto the backyard.

67

Also on the ground level were the kitchen in the back and a powder room in the hallway. In the front was a small room, which the sisters called the organ room because it housed a pipe organ. As in most Dutch houses, there was no finished basement—just a cellar that one entered through a door in the hallway. Upstairs, in front, was a large bedroom for Bets and Ann, a music room in the back, a bathroom above the kitchen. Another small room in front became my bedroom. A large attic ran over the entire width and length of the house.

A fence and a high hedge closed off a narrow strip of garden to the right side of the house, so that from the street one couldn't be seen in the backyard. The front yard was only ten feet deep and bordered by a two-foot high brick wall. A short driveway to the left of the house led to a one-car garage and to the front door. The garage was used to store the tandem and a specially constructed bicycle for four. We had used it twice that summer and people in the street stopped to stare at us riding on that strange contraption. Bets and Ann rode as if in rapture, their faces up at a slight angle, always that angle.

There was no house to our immediate left, but to our right, on the corner of Rembrandt Avenue and Nassau Avenue, stood the house of Mr. Loopstra. He had been a teacher at my high school and was now the Director of the Gymnasium, the grammar school. From his upstairs bedroom, he looked down on our back garden, but he wouldn't betray me if he ever saw me. Although he taught German, his sympathies were entirely against the Nazis. Opposite the two houses was the MULO School.

The two sisters were excited by my arrival, but there was no time to lose. I had to get a new identity. Ann, who had suggested that I could masquerade as a blind person, offered to discuss it with the Director of the Institute for the Blind.

"I trust him completely. He always has given me good advice," she said.

Trust went a long way during the war. Everybody knew a few people they could trust implicitly and depend on in time of need. Ann, who had depended so much on others all her life, placed her complete trust in the Director. He had seen me several times and when Ann arrived with a new driver, he probably realized that it was I she was referring to when she approached him. He told her that the "person" would need a new identity paper and indicated that he knew how to get one. He had told Ann that the "person" would have to choose a new name and that evening we had fun making up all sorts of names. It was Bets who came up with the best one.

"I have an idea," she said. "Why don't we make it Stern? It's the German word for 'star'.

"Not bad, the Jews wear a star and Stern can even be a Jewish name," I said. "That'll confuse them if they ever see me with that name. An uncircumcised, red-haired Dutchman with a Jewish name."

"And we can even use the same letters for a first name, Ernst," Ann added.

We had made our choice. Two days later, a man came to the house, who didn't introduce himself, spoke only a few words, took my picture and a print of my thumb and index finger, and left.

Having the right documents during the war could make a difference between life and death. The underground soon started making false identification papers and, ironically, the Germans, with their love for bureaucracy, helped considerably. Their numerous documents often required one or more seals or stamps to attest for the authenticity of the documents and for this they had recruited the services of The Royal Stamp Factory of J.D.Posthumus in Amsterdam, one of few firms in Europe specializing in the making of dies for stamps.

69

The German Occupation Force became its largest client in 1940. Posthumus not only made the stamps, but also printed documents on the special paper provided by the Germans. Unbeknownst to their client, the firm kept extra samples of the stamps and the paper, which they put to good use for the Dutch underground. The beauty of these stamps was that they could not be identified as forgeries. They were real. The most important document by far was the identity card, which everybody above the age of fourteen had to carry on their person at all times. The Dutch card was a technical marvel and considered fraud resistant. It showed a photograph of the carrier, two fingerprints, a watermark, two official stamps, and a signature, and it cost one guilder. Jacobus Lambertus Lentz, Chief Inspector of the Dutch National Citizen Register, had designed the three-part document. Lentz, a German sympathizer and anti-Semite, had thought of everything. He not only used special paper, but also ink that became invisible under quartz light and was sensitive to solvents. The card for a Jew was marked with a big black ' J.'

Many attempts were made to falsify this identity card, but the results were often rather poor. J.F.Duwaer, a printer, collaborated with the sculptor Gerrit J. van der Veen in producing some seventy thousand false documents, by far the best made. Their artist was the designer Otto Treumann, a German-born Jew who lived in Amsterdam. Treumann managed to copy the most intricate part of the document, the watermark. Sem Hartz, also a Jew, copied the signatures to perfection, even that of Rauter, the highest ranked SS officer in Holland.

A week after the mysterious man had taken my photograph and fingerprints, I received my new card, marked A35 / No. 625825, issued on January 16, 1942 to Stern, Ernst Eduard, born on the 15th of January, 1927 in Wageningen, and now living on Amstellaan 15 III in Amsterdam. My occupation was student. The watermark is visible on all three parts, the thumb print was initialed by EV 102. The 'official' who signed my card was G.J.van der Veen. We found the card that evening behind the door under the mail slot after someone had rung the doorbell. I signed it "E. Stern." *

Ann took the identity card to the Institute where the Director used it to write a letter that stated that Ernst E. Stern, identity card A35/No.625825, was a student at the Institute for the Blind. In addition to the identity card, every able-bodied Dutchman between the ages of fifteen and fifty was also required to carry an Ausweis, a document showing that the holder had been registered for the "Arbeitseinsatz" and had permission to work in Holland in a job which the Germans found essential for their war effort. It made the holder of an Ausweis exempt from deportation to Germany. The older boys in the Institute didn't need an Ausweis. The Germans had no use for them.

My dad also didn't need an Ausweis. He had a little talk with an old classmate, a man he shared a drink with now and then in one of the pubs he frequented. This man was a town hall clerk and after the talk, he changed Dad's year of birth from 1898 to 1890 and entered it as such in the official town registry.

The first few days on Rembrandt Avenue number 35 were full of surprises for the sisters, as well as for me. It began with an inspection of me.

"We want to know what you look like," Ann said.

They looked me over in the only way they knew how, by taking turns feeling my face, touching lips, nose, eyes, ears and hair, making comments as they went along. "Oh, you wear glasses." I had a good face, they concluded, a wide mouth and thick hair. I just stood in the middle of the room not quite knowing how to react. At first there

---

*Treumann and Hartz survived the war, but Duwear and van der Veen were caught and executed by the Germans.

71

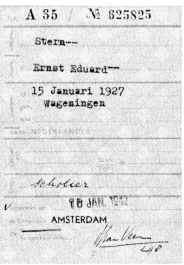

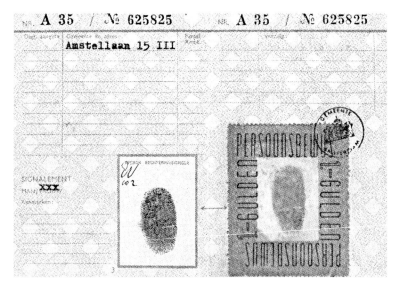

The false identity card

was embarassment especially when I had to bend down to the much smaller Bets.

"I can't reach you," she said.

However, the embarrassment soon gave way to amusement when I noticed how perfectly natural it was for these two middle-aged women. My shoulders were not very wide for a man they thought, but my belly was flat, which for some reason they liked. They once more said that they liked the color of my hair. It seemed strange that they were interested in colors.

"You have strong hands with long fingers, good for playing the piano," Ann said.

"Can I feel your chest?" Bets asked.

"What?"

"I want to feel your chest." She was dead serious.

I unbuttoned my shirt, bent over, and she felt inside.

"You have no hair on your chest," she said, amazed.

"Bets! Behave," Ann exclaimed when she realized what Bets had done. Bets shrugged.

"I heard that men have hair on their chest and I wanted to see what it feels like," she said dryly. "Why don't you have hair on your chest, Barth?"

"I don't know. I just never had."

"I like you better without it," said Ann, but the logic of her remark escaped me. She hadn't felt it. After the inspection was over, they gave me a tour of the house, starting with my bedroom.

"We'll start with your room," Ann said.

"Is the bed long enough?" Bets asked.

I tried it out and my feet stuck out over the end, but I made no mention of it.

The three of us living together initially presented a few problems. It was the first time that the two women had a man living with them and they needed to make some adjustments, as did I. At ages fifty-four and fifty-two, they ran around in

73

their long nightgowns, noisy and giggling like teenagers. There were no locks on the doors and on the second day, Bets walked into the bathroom pulling her nightgown over her head, when she suddenly realized that I was already there. "Oops," she yelled and retreated to tell her sister. Boisterous laughter followed. A few days later, I, too, made a similar mistake of not knocking before entering the bathroom, only to find Ann naked in the tub.

"Oh, I am sorry," I stammered.

"Don't worry, you could see worse." She laughed with those typical short bursts. Shyness was unnatural for both women.

I soon learned that they hated the word 'blind.' They revolted against it, against the notion that they were incomplete, that there was something missing in them.

"Being blind is not the end of the world," Bets said. "People forget that we have all the other senses. Mentally and spiritually we probably see better than they do."

As a result of the unexpected encounters in the bathroom, we made some rules, which included singing or whistling to make one's presence known. In the morning, Ann, who had to leave for the Institute, used the bathroom first, then Bets and I came last. At night, Bets went first, followed by Ann, and again I was last. After breakfast and Ann had left for the Institute, I went upstairs to make my bed and clean my room, what little of it there was. A chair, small table and a bookshelf. But no books. Who needed books in the house of the blind?

When Bets was not giving piano lessons in the upstairs music room, she usually was downstairs in her favorite chair, the one with the stool, reading a book, her fingers moving rapidly over the Braille dots. The books were huge, easily measuring twelve by eighteen inches, and the pages were made of thick, firm, light brown paper. It had to be firm, otherwise the little raised dots of the Braille would soon collapse. It took three to five books in Braille to translate one typeset book. Bets rarely read with the book lying on the table. She preferred having it on her lap, her feet on the footstool. With hands moving over the pages and her head tilted up at that slight angle to the left, she was a picture of tranquility, of inner peace. The blinking of her eyelids was the only other movement. The house came alive when Ann returned in the evening. Then there were stories to tell and laughter to share. It was a happy house.

"Ann, why don't you ask one of your students to bring you a large map of Europe and a box with colored pins," I said soon after I moved in.

"What for?"

"You'll see. I'll show you and Bets how the war progresses."

The first couple of times that I said, "You'll see," I had checked myself, but now all three of us were using the phrase. Practically every family in Holland had a map on the wall and I would have been surprised if the same wasn't true in the other occupied countries. Ann didn't wait for a student to bring one in. The next day, she brought one from the Institute. The Director hadn't batted an eye when she asked for it and for several boxes with pins. From then on, he also gave her newspapers to read.

"Ask your housekeeper to read them to you."

I pasted the map on a piece of cardboard and fixed it on the wall of the dining room, opposite the door. I used small pins for the original borders of Germany, Poland, Russia, and other countries, and larger ones to outline the Russian front. There may have been a map in every Dutch family, but without a doubt ours had the most pins.

The sisters hadn't felt the borders of the countries of Europe since they were teenagers and had to learn them all over again before they appreciated where the front line was. They had a good idea how the Germans had overrun their neighboring countries, Holland, Belgium, France and Denmark. All they had to do was to cross a border, but their occupation of Norway needed some explaining. The expansion to the East was a revelation for them, because, before they felt the pins, they had no idea of the enormous distances.

"They must need every German to occupy all that land. No wonder they need slave labor to work in their factories," Ann said.

"They'll never be able to keep all that land. It's too much," Bets added.

Even though the Dutch newspapers and radio stations were completely under German control, it was nevertheless possible to patch the true situation together from those two sources as well as from the BBC and from word of mouth. The German propaganda machine always managed to put a positive twist on German losses, but we ignored the twists and only used the facts.

"People who are strong enough to bear the loss of Stalingrad and, yes, who gain extra strength from it, can not be defeated."

These were the words from that smooth-tongued propaganda-minister Goebbels when he addressed his henchmen in the Berlin Sports Palace soon after the German army had been annihilated in Stalingrad. Throughout the battle we were fed similar nonsense, but we distilled the truth from it by reading between the lines. The phrase "Victorious German troops" was gradually replaced with "Courageous German troops," which was a seemingly small difference, but to us the change from "victorious" to "courageous" was a significant one. Phrases such as "elastic repositioning of German troops" and "strategic shortening of the frontline" were accompanied by the naming of towns, which meant that we had to change the position of our pins. That way, we learned that the Germans were retreating. And if they were late in acknowledging the loss of yet another town, the BBC was ready to fill us in.

The sisters loved that map, especially Bets. Almost daily, I saw her standing in front of it. She talked softly to herself as she followed the lines of pins with both hands. Sometimes a pin fell out. She tried to find it on the floor and if she did, searched for the spot from which it had fallen. Most of the time she succeeded. It took her a while, and I purposely didn't help her.

Another indication that the Germans were losing the war was the increasing number of obituaries of Dutch volunteers at the Russian front. The same paper that reported the attack on Seyffardt, printed the obituaries of Dirk Hemelop, age 19, and of Frans van de Boon, age 23. "They offered their young lives for the Führer, Volk and Vaderland," their death notices read. Bets, who normally abhorred all violence, actually looked forward to me reading these announcements.

"Good, the more the better. We don't need those traitors," she said, without a trace of pity.

In more ways than one, Bets reminded me of Mother, who had also gone through so many tough times. I remember how happy Mother was when we moved once again, to Number 80 Egelantierstraat, a corner house on a block of eight. She now had a garden in front, on one side, and in the back. When she came home with her bicycle, she no longer had to use the common path behind the other houses to reach our shed. The family had moved up in the world. The house had the same number of rooms as the one on the Iris Street, but here the stairs separated the living room from the front room— the one I was given for my study. It had no heat and no electricity. During the winter months, I wrapped a blanket around me and warmed my hands on the oil lamp. Every hour or so, I went into the living room to warm my feet.

77

Mother rarely if ever bought something for herself. Her clothes were remakes from dresses discarded by the ladies of the houses in which she worked, or she picked them out at the Salvation Army. She also made most of our clothes. Mother had two little secrets. She turned over every penny and each penny saved went into the flowerpot on the mantelpiece, the secret all of us knew about. But she used that pot mainly as a decoy. She kept a second jar under her bed and that we didn't know about. Her son was soon going to the university and Mother decided that the green velvet jacket and pants with the stain would no longer do. When the time arrived, she emptied the jar under her bed, took me to the department store, and selected a new suit from the rack for the enormous price of forty-eight guilders, or thirteen dollars and thirty cents at the exchange rate of that time. It was my first suit. Lectures at the Medical School in Utrecht started in September. I had been given the one scholarship the town of Hilversum gave each year to a deserving student. When Jan de Wijn, the Nazi Youth leader in our last high school class, found out about it, he demanded the scholarship for himself and it was taken away from me. It was the end of my hopes of going to medical school. However, three weeks later, de Wijn had another calling. He volunteered for the Russian front and I was in again. Together, with three fellow students, I hopped the train to Utrecht six days a week. We stored our bikes in the shed of the small adjunct station and usually came racing down when the train had already come to a stop. Groeneveld, the shed keeper, was waiting for us. We jumped off our bikes at full speed, he caught them, and we raced to catch the train. Only once during that year did I miss the train. We were the railroad students, unlike other students who rented rooms in Utrecht.

The scholarship only paid for the tuition. For the rest, my family scraped together every penny. A guilder and a half a week for bicycle storage, twelve guilders a month for the train, money for secondhand books, paper and pens, a kit to dissect frogs and other animals. The microscope was by far the most expensive item. Dad insisted that I buy a good one, a monocular Leitz, a beautiful shiny instrument in a light colored wooden carrying case. Not all students had such a good-looking case. I carried it with pride. It was my status symbol, our family's status symbol. We must have been the only student family to think that way about a wooden box. Dad had borrowed some of the money for the microscope from friends, including his partner Piet and Uncle Jaap, who were just as proud that I was going to medical school. Coos chipped in from her savings and Mother emptied her not-so- secret hiding place, the flowerpot on the mantelpiece. It was a family affair.

6

Living with Bets and Ann

"We have decided that you must study music, otherwise, you'll get bored to death," Ann said and Bets agreed. They had talked it over and so I began with piano and flute lessons, both given by Ann. We sat together on the wide piano stool, she on the right, and she told me to take a book of sheet music from the top of a pile that was always in the same spot on the far left side of the piano.

"When you finish with it, you must put it back in the same place you took it from. I know the exact order and if we keep it in that order I can always tell my students which one to take."

From years of experience, the sisters had worked out this nearly perfect system. It never failed with the older students and since the little ones were too small to reach the top of the piano, Ann put it back herself. Occasionally, a student put a piece of music in the wrong place and Ann patiently had to go through the pile with the next student. After the first five lessons, if the student or the parent of a little one decided to continue with the lessons, they were expected to buy their own music.

Ann took me through the first lesson.

"Open the first page and tell me what you see."

"I see five lines and eight notes. Some are on a line and some between the lines."

"Good. Those note are called a scale, starting with a C at the bottom."

She sang the scale and demonstrated the same scale on the piano. She took my right hand, placed hers lightly on top of it, put my thumb on the C, and demonstrated how that thumb had to move under the other fingers in order to play an entire scale. In the beginning, her left hand was always on top of my right hand, feather light, not interfering with the motion of my fingers. When I was more advanced, she listened and only stopped me when her sharp ears detected a wrong positioning of my fingers. Back came her hand and "Do that again," followed by the inevitable correction. With never-ending patience, she demonstrated difficult passages until I had it right. I enjoyed those lessons. The closeness of her on the piano stool gave me a pleasant feeling, a warm feeling.

It went the same way with the flute. She put my fingers in the correct position and pulled a recalcitrant pinky far out to a valve near the end of the flute. She pursed her lower lip and folded the upper lip over it, leaving a narrow opening. "That is the embouchure," she explained.

I had all the time in the world to practice and was a fast learner. Bets never corrected me during practice, but now and then she did comment, always in an encouraging way. "That was very nice." She leaned over the arm of her chair when she said it, looking in my direction. Later, they bought an old cello for me. It made a beautiful sound, and although there was nobody to teach me, it became my favorite instrument. After a few months, I had advanced enough with the flute so that we could form a trio, with Bets playing the violin and Ann the piano. We sounded pretty good after a while, so good, in fact, that on Sunday mornings we began to have an audience. The school across the street was first occupied by a unit of the Waffen SS and later by the Grüne Polizei, the tough German military police. One Sunday morning, I saw a

81

German soldier sitting on the little wall of the front garden, listening to us play.

"Hey, we have an audience. There is a German sitting on the wall outside."

"Maybe he likes music," Ann said.

Later, there were two and eventually four or five. One time, they actually applauded and we pantomimed our part, bowing. The sisters never worried about our amazing audience, Germans, our enemy. They couldn't see them, so they might as well not have been there. They felt secure in the confinement of their blind world, didn't see the hated uniform. In the seeing world, they were occasionally helpless, a helplessness that made them vulnerable, momentarily dependent on others, having to trust them. Over the years they had learned that people could be trusted and after being given assistance, they thanked them and moved safely back into their own world. So they smiled when they pantomimed and the Germans smiled back. Humans with feelings, lonely, away from home and family. If only they didn't wear that uniform. With it, they felt strong. Without it, they were just like ordinary people and equally vulnerable.

"You know, they are not superhuman." I said out of the blue sky.

"What brought that up all of a sudden?" Ann asked.

"Oh, I was just thinking about something that happened two years ago in the indoor swimming pool. My brother and I each had a water polo ball and were taking twenty laps of the pool propelling us with the legs only. Our trainer, Jan Stender, was busy with a few other swimmers, when two Germans in swim trunks showed up. They looked like any other swimmer, naked except for a small piece of cloth. Suddenly, one of them dove in the water, pushed my brother under, and took his ball away. I got mad, swam towards him, pushed him under and then, using a water polo trick, clamped his head between my legs. Only when he was really struggling did I let him go. He came up gasping for air and scampered to the edge of the pool. Jaap and I continued our laps as if nothing had happened. In the meanwhile, the two Germans got dressed and they were waiting for me when I came out of the water. One of them yelled at me and grabbed my arm. Stender, a bear of a man with a body covered with hair, saw what was going on. He rushed over and let loose a torrent of words at the two soldiers. He dressed them down worse than their sergeant could ever have done. And they left, just like that. You see, without their uniforms, they were naked and vulnerable. The uniform gave them the courage to harass me, but they slunk away when Stender raised his voice."

"They are only grown-up boys," Bets mused.

"Those boys can be very nasty. You were lucky that your trainer was around," Ann said.

"Exercise; you must have exercise." Again Ann took the initiative. "We'll walk in the garden. Let's go."

The garden in the back of the house measured about thirty by forty feet. It was a simple garden, walled off by the house and garage on two sides and an eight-foot-high wooden fence on the other sides. There were bushes along the fences, but most of the garden consisted of a square lawn bordered by a gravel path. Ann and I walked the path, arm in arm, faster and faster, around and around, twenty, thirty, fifty times. We did it every day, rain or shine. That was our exercise. Bets never joined us. I began to have the feeling that, when the three of us were together, she tended to let Ann do most of the interacting with me. One bright sunny afternoon, Ann suddenly stopped in mid-walk. She cocked her head sideways, neck stretched, and cried out, "I see something!"

Holding her head in that peculiar, awkward way, she bent over and ever so slowly moved over the grass, sideways like a crab. Finally, she crouched down until her head was one foot away from a small piece of glass in the grass. Incredibly, a minute ray of sunshine had reflected in that one spot of her left eye through which she inexplicably experienced a light sensation. Never, in her entire life, had anything like that happened before, not even when the many doctors had examined her. She tried to pick up the piece of glass, but couldn't direct her hand to the right spot. The shadow of her hand blocked the sun out and she lost the reflection.

"I can't touch it," she cried out.

"I know, it's too small. But you saw it, didn't you?"

I tried to help her in the moment that she wanted it all, the seeing and the touching. We were both very excited.

"Let me try it again."

She held her hands, fists to her mouth in an enormously strong emotion. And we tried it again, starting out from the exact same spot on the path. Ann's entire body tensed up and her face took on an expression of fierce determination. The muscles in her neck tightened as she moved her head in minute motions. Sideways, up a little, tilting, stretching, holding. Another adjustment, and then she held her head motionless in that same skewed, awkward position. She had it again. She repeated the same crab-like walk, crouching, and head dead still. This time I helped her pick up the piece of glass. We both crouched down on the grass.

"Put your thumb and index finger so that they form a circle," I instructed her.

I took her hand, moved it until the shadow of the circle was around the piece of glass, and then, ever so carefully pushed her hand down until she felt the grass.

"Now the glass is in the middle of the circle. Try touching it."

And she did. Her tense body relaxed and she stood up. Only then could she smile. A miracle had happened.

"I don't know what to say. It's ... it is ... I ... ah ...."

For once in her life, Ann was speechless. She slowly shook

her head, her shoulders sagged, and it was as if all air left her body. After a long pause, she took control of herself.

"Let's see whether Bets can also find it."

I went to fetch Bets. For a long time, that small figure stood on the path, moving her head slowly at every possible angle, but Bets never saw it and after about an hour we gave up. I felt intensely sorry for her. That evening, the excitement was still palpable. Bets naturally was disappointed, but she was happy for Ann.

"I have lived in darkness so long that I wouldn't know what to do if I could suddenly see." She shrugged her small shoulders. "The sunlight would probably blind me." She laughed at her own joke, but it didn't come out quite right.

"From now on you must try every day when the sun shines," she said to Ann.

The piece of glass was too small to find routinely and instead I used a pillow covered with a light blue, satin-like material. Thrown anywhere on the grass it reflected the sunlight very well and from more than one angle. Ann, head cocked and neck stretched, moved and moved until she caught a glimpse of reflecting light and then walked the same crab-like walk to the pillow. It became part of our routine. On overcast days, we walked around the little lawn and on sunny days we looked for the pillow.

Walking the path and going twice a day to fill the coalscuttle from the bin in the garage were my only exercises. Because they ran a school, the sisters received extra coal rations and they didn't have to worry about keeping their house warm. It was different in my home and one evening I told Bets and Ann how my dad had solved that problem.

"I'll call the story Prutten."

"Prutten? What does that mean?" Ann said.

"You never heard of it?"

"No."

85

"It sound a little like some noise," Bets said.

"You are close, Bets. But let me tell you the story and when I'm finished you'll know what prutten means. It happened early last year."

"Look boy, a rabbit."

Jan Rempe and I were walking through the heavy dewed grass. The sun had yet to come up from behind the tree line at the far end of the meadow and the sky still hung dark in the west. A cow looked up curiously at us, while others kept on grazing, their large heads low to the ground, backs straight, thick veins crisscrossing the soft pink of their swollen udders. The morning stillness was broken only by the sloshing of our boots and by the swish of wet grass as the cows pulled it from its roots. One animal curved its back, lifted its tail and soft, green dung plopped to the ground, first in large blobs, spattering, then smaller blobs and a last one. The tail came slowly down, the back straightened. The cow never stopped grazing. We avoided the fresh piles of manure as we walked, a leg swinging aside at the last moment. Not that it mattered much if we stepped into one, because the wet grass would clean our hip boots soon enough, but a fresh heap could be mighty slippery and an unaware city man could easily spread-eagle or fall on his behind. Farmers had fun with that. It gave them something to talk about for a week or so.

"Where? I don't see a rabbit," I said.

"Straight ahead. See its white tail?"

Jan, who towered over me, had the eyes of an eagle. Just then the rabbit looked up, pricked its ears and hopped away, unhurried. Now I also saw it, about fifty yards away.

"How can you see that far?" I said. "Sun isn't even up."

"You got to learn one thing boy—a good poacher has to see before being seen."

Jan, who couldn't read or write, was a good poacher.

———

"Hardly ever been caught, he was," the people of Loosdrecht said. "He is the best."

He kept walking in long, easy strides forcing me to take an extra step now and then to keep up. Big, effortless strides that ate the ground without making a sound, the seemingly slow walk of a good poacher, the best. At the end of the meadow, we went through the swing gate and followed the narrow path along the creek. Ten-foot high reeds crowned with feathery plumes bent overhead. Large dewdrops clung to the tall grasses and our boots and shirts soon got thoroughly wet. Dew makes good drinking when you are thirsty and we paused to take a few licks.

"Cleanest water on earth, boy."

He had always called me 'boy,' ever since I was a youngster. The row boat, tied to one of the blinds Dad and Jan used for duck hunting in the spring and fall, lay waiting at the end of the creek, where it opened up into the lake. Dad had made that boat about a dozen years ago and it was still in good shape with not a leak in it. The little water at the bottom was leftover rain most likely.

Jan rowed us to where a flat boat was moored to two long poles, a couple of hundred yards into the lake. The oars pushed the waterlilies aside as we moved along. A frog jumped from one of the large leaves. It was still too early in the day for the flowers to open their white petals and show their yellow-gold center.

"You and Jan Rempe go prutten next week," Dad had said the day after I finished the final exam of my high school. "We'll need peat to heat the house come winter." It was spring of 1942 and the Germans had already rationed the coal to heat our houses. They confiscated most of it for themselves. 'Für das Vaterland,' they said, just as they stole our butter, cheese, the best animals, and whatever else they could lay their hands on. Dad and Jan grew up together in Loosdrecht and they knew the old ways. Knew how to make peat briquettes just like the farmers used to make them centuries ago. They used the same old tools and spoke the same old words.

We stepped on the wide sideboard of the flat boat and I hung the bottles with cold tea over the side. The sun was up now, its rays shimmering on the smooth water.

"It's going to be a hot one, boy."

Jan never said much. He was a bachelor, not the marrying type. He lived with his Ma and Pa and his sister in a small, two-bedroom house on the side of the only road in Loosdrecht. It had an open pit toilet in the back, forty feet away, at the edge of the ditch. They lived from the odd jobs Jan did for farmers or the squire and from what Sister brought in. During the summer months, his Ma sold eel, which Jan caught and his Pa smoked. In crude letters the sign said, 'Smoked eel for sale.' Sister had painted it and Jan had nailed it to the tree next to the road. It hung crooked. Same old weathered sign hung there all year round, five, ten years . . . always crooked. In the fall, Jan snared rabbits on the lands of the squire. Sometimes, on a late Saturday night, when he knew that the gamekeeper was drunk, with the help of a few too many rounds of Jenever, Jan would shoot a deer. As I said, Jan was a bachelor. When he felt the need, and when he had the money, he went into town and found himself a woman in a bar. But that didn't happen too often—only when he felt the need and when he had the money.

"Yep, it's going to be a hot one."

Jan talked as he walked, slow and easy, with pauses. Never in a hurry. He spoke like men of the land do all over the world, looking at the horizon, chewing a sprig of grass in a corner of the mouth and spitting saliva. The land wasn't in a hurry, so why should he be?

"Better get to work," he said.

We untied the flatboat, pulled the stakes, and pushed the heavy boat to another spot where Jan planted the stakes deep in the mud and tied up the boat. He lifted a thirty-foot long, three-inch thick pole with a heavy steel hoop at the end from which a large net hung. Over the side it went and he dragged the net over the bottom of the lake while walking the full length of the boat. He then lifted the net, filled with partly decayed plant matter, out of the water and emptied it in the boat. I could hardly lift the pole itself, let alone when the net was full. Only a huge, strong man like Jan could do it, hour after hour. I had to get rid of the excess water and help move the boat now and then. It was a big boat—ten feet across, easily forty feet long and two feet deep.

Come eleven o'clock, it was time to eat the sandwiches Jan had brought. In his farming community, he still had access to dark brown bread with butter and thick slices of smoked bacon without a thread of meat in it, from the fattest pigs. We drank the cold tea as we ate.

Sitting there on the side of the flatboat, we looked at God's beautiful world. Sailboats drifted lazily in the water, their white sails standing out against the green, tree-lined borders of the lake. A farmer pulled the oars of his black tarred rowboat, on his way to somewhere..two large milk cans in the bow. In the far distance, the sun reflected on the steeple of the twelfth-century church in which I had been baptized. Birds raced through the blue sky, coots broke the water surface, leaving ever widening rings in a mirror. A lone heron stood motionless on the nearby shore.

"Better get back to work," Jan broke the silence.

It was hot now and he took his thick woolen shirt off, but not the long-sleeved underwear folks of the land always wore, winter and summer. Only his face, neck, and hands were deeply tanned and weather beaten. His forehead, where his cap covered it, was bone white.

We worked in silence until the boat lay deep in the water, filled with sweet smelling, half rotten, black goo in which the outline of leaves and stems could still be recognized after hundreds of years in the water. We pulled the stakes and slowly pushed the heavy flatboat to the shore. Small waves from a distant motor boat lapped over the side. Jan steered us to a piece of land about the size of the boat. It sloped ever so slightly toward the water. A couple of days ago, he and Dad had cleared the shrub away, leaving only two young trees to which we tied the boat.

We each took a strange-looking shovel that had been carved from a single piece of wood many years ago. The scoop was sixteen inches long, about nine inches wide, and it had a flat bottom. Beginning at the end of the scoop, the side sloped up and around, reaching five inches high in the center. Jan showed me how to use it. Standing knee-deep in the mud with feet planted wide apart, his knees at a comfortable angle and with his back bent at sixty degrees, he moved the shovel in a half circle. Back and forth, down through the mud and up and twist and down again, all in one continuous motion. His back never came up; only his massive shoulders turned when he brought the shovel up and twisted the scoop so that the mud flew from it and spread out on the land, in blobs. I tried it, awkward at first, but then got the hang of it and we worked hour after hour. The level of mud in the boat came down slowly and, on the land, it started to get some depth. As the blobs fell, they began to make a peculiar sound, something like cow manure plopping down from under a raised tail. But it wasn't exactly a 'plop' sound; more like 'prrrrt, prrrrt'.

"Hear that sound, boy? That's why we call it prutten."

When the late evening sun dipped once again behind the trees, we had finished our work and the wet peat lay thick on the land. And I couldn't straighten up. I dropped the shovel, put both hands in the small of my back and slowly, painfully came up.

"It'll be easier tomorrow," Jan grinned.

He rowed us to the blind and we walked back through

the meadow. The cows were down, chewing their cud. I had trouble getting on my bike.

"It'll be easier tomorrow," Dad grinned when I came home.

Only it wasn't. He woke me up early in the morning and I rode my bike to Loosdrecht, stiff as a rod, blisters on both hands. It was easier on the third day, and at the end of the fourth day, we had enough peat on the land, just when I began to feel like an old hand. There it lay, slowly drying out. In September, Jan and Dad used the old peat cutters to make briquettes, which I stacked in piles.

"That was a nice story," Bets said when I was finished. "I can see that cow before me. And the frog."

She saw the animals.

"How big were those briquettes and did you use them?" Ann wanted to know.

"They were about one foot long and four inches wide and high. They give off tremendous heat, but you have to be careful to close the stove immediately after you add a couple, because they cause a lot of smoke."

"Amazing. We knew that there were lakes in Loosdrecht, but had no idea how they came about," Bets said. "I learned something."

The blindness brought on some delicate situations now that there was a man in the house, not so much for the sisters as for me. Bets returned from the toilet one day with the hem of her skirt caught in the elastic band of her underpants. I looked at it, hoping that it would adjust itself as she sat down, but it didn't. Only then did I have the courage to tell her.

"Bets, your skirt isn't all the way down." It sounded awkward, but I wasn't brave enough to tell her that her panties showed.

"Thank you," she said and pulled the skirt out. That was

91

it . . . simple. It happened a few more times during the course of the year, and all I then said was, "You are showing off your sex again."

"Oops," was the standard reply.

"Ann, you have a piece of spinach on your teeth."

"Thank you, Barth," she replied and removed the piece from the corner of her front tooth.

Their father had taught the girls to use the tjebok bottol, a bottle filled with water, to cleanse themselves in the bathroom, just like he had learned from the people in the Far East. It was cheaper and more hygienic than toilet paper, and so the two sisters and I splashed water to clean our behinds and then washed our hands in the little sink. There was one serious drawback to this method—the water felt very cold during the winter months. It could happen that a piece of dried feces remained stuck in the rim of a fingernail and I would tell them. At first, I was too embarrassed to say something, but then I realized how awkward it would be when they gave piano lessons. What thoughts went through the minds of the pupils when they noticed it, I wondered. So I told them and they washed their hands again and thanked me. It was all so natural, so normal.

"Bets, wipe your moustache," I would say when she had a rim of milk on her upper lip. Little things like that. I wondered how often other people had not alerted them to such things. Had they been too embarrassed to say something? If only they had known that neither sister ever felt ill at ease by it.

Bets and Ann never used a white cane. As far as I knew, there wasn't even one in the house. Over the years, they had walked into numerous objects and had the scars to show for it. At home, we had strict rules. Doors were either closed or completely open, never halfway open, and the furniture had to remain in the exact same place all the time. A cleaning lady came the house on Tuesday and Friday mornings and during that time I locked myself in my room and remained quiet as a mouse. She was told not to bother with that little room. When, after vacuuming one day, a new maid left a chair in a wrong spot, Bets, walking fast as usual, ran into it and hurt her shinbone rather badly. "Stupid woman," Bets mumbled. A new scar.

When the house was first build and sold to the sisters, the builder had to make one concession for their blindness—he had to change all the light switches. Normally people turned the switch on or off with a continuous clockwork turn, but that wouldn't work for blind people. He changed them to up-down switches, up for light on and down for light out. That way there never was any confusion when the last sister to go to bed checked all the lights.

Ann still went to the Institute four times a week, but now a woman was driving her. She rang the bell in the morning and waited outside for Ann. I never met her, but she knew that there was a young man in the house from a little game Ann and I played every morning. When they left and drove past in front of the house, I opened the window and hit one key on the grand piano. Ann would either smile triumphantly when she knew the key or, less often, she would frown. Coming home that evening she would tell me which key I had struck. Rarely was she wrong, and then only one key off. When asked, Ann told her new driver that I was a blind nephew living with them.

"Bets, I'd like you to teach me Braille," I asked during the second month on Rembrandt Avenue.

"Why do you want to learn that?" she said.

"Oh, I might as well make myself useful. Converting music into Braille or something like that."

When Ann studied for a recital she often had to wait a long time for the music to come from the National Organization for the Blind, where scores were converted into Braille. A regular music score was much easier to obtain and I figured that I might be able to help her if I converted that music into Braille for her.

Bets first explained the system. The entire Braille language consists of only six raised dots, which, when pressed in sturdy paper, can easily be felt with the tips of the fingers. They are arranged in clusters, two dots across and three dots down and numbered 1, 2 and 3 on the left, and 4, 5 and 6 on the right side. For instance, the letter "a" is the number one dot in the left upper corner, the B is numbers 1 and 2, and the Y is numbers 1,3,4,5 and 6. With these six dots one can translate almost anything, including calculus and music. The sisters wrote in Braille either by hand or with a typewriter. By hand, they used a metal slide, which was as long as the width of the paper and about two inches wide. It consisted of two parts, with a hinge on the left side. The bottom half of the steel slide was full of small, round hollows, arranged in clusters of six and the clusters were further arranged in three rows of about thirty each. The paper was held in place with short, sharp spines at the top corners of the bottom half and then the top half closed over the paper. This half had three rows of rectangular openings, with round indentations along all four sides of the opening, again two across and three down, forming a cluster. These indentations corresponded exactly with the six hollows of each cluster in the bottom half. Using a wooden ball with a steel pin at one end, the writer put the pin into the desired impression and pushed down on the paper below, forming a dot. It was cumbersome work because one could only press one dot at a time and some letters consisted of four or more dots. In addition, after every three lines, the paper had to be moved up. Even the sisters, whose hands raced over the slide, took a long time to write a letter. It went much faster with the typewriter. That device had no keyboard, only six inch-long keys, and three for each hand. They were set in a horizontal line so that the fingers didn't have to move up or down while typing. The paper moved as in a regular typewriter, which was another great improvement.

After she had explained the Braille system, Bets went through the alphabet with me and typed out the music notes, as well as the figures. That first day, I tried the slide and pick method, and it was very slow going. After a couple of hours, my hand began to hurt and I stopped. "My hand hurts," I said. Bets laughed. "When I was young, we only had the pick and we used it all day in school. Here, feel my hand."

After all these years, there was still a bony hard swelling at the base of her index finger, the result of long hours of holding the pick when she was a child.

"Let me show you how the typewriter works."

Bets sat next to me, closer than she had ever been before. I felt a distinct change in her when she took my hands and guided the three middle fingers to the keys. Before, Ann had done all the teaching and Bets had let us, in an offish sort of way. Now it was different. It was her turn. She took charge of me and I enjoyed the growing closer together.

With the mechanical device, I first copied part of the newspaper and Bets complimented me—only four errors. There was one problem with the machine—in order to make a correction, one had to wait until the page was finished, then read the page, turn the paper up side down, push the offending dot back and make a new one with the pick. Next, I practiced writing music, which took a longer time to learn because I was on less familiar ground. I made more mistakes and it took at least three times as long to learn as the alphabet. But I became proficient enough so that when the sisters decided to attend a performance of 'The Lohengrin' by Wagner, I offered to convert the entire libretto in Braille so that they could follow it along with the singers. Working all day, it took me four weeks to complete my task, just in time for opera night. I made two sets and there was no such thing as a copying machine. It was nice to see the sisters leave, dressed in their Sunday best, each with two thick books under their arms. They were serenely happy, their faces glowed, their chins up.

"You should try to read Braille with your fingers, without looking," Bets challenged me a few days after the opera.

It was easy to feel one or two dots, but it took a while to distinguish letters consisting of four or five dots from each other with the tip of one finger. With words, I first had to identify each letter, before figuring out what it was. But I kept at it and was amazed how sensitive my index finger became when I put my mind to it. Of course, I hadn't used my hands for any hard labor in a long time and they were as soft as silk, which helped in feeling the dots. I still used only that one finger, whereas the sisters used eight, something I never did master. But I did succeed in identifying letters and numbers with each index finger, which speeded up the process of reading a word. After a while, I could at long last read parts of a book, to the great delight of the sisters.

"Now you really can act as a blind person," Bets said proudly. My next step in getting familiar with their world was to try going blindfolded for part of the day. Just keeping my eyes shut wasn't enough to enter that world, because, even with my eyes closed, I still noticed the difference between darkness and light through my eyelids. I also was tempted to cheat when I couldn't find a door opening soon enough. Putting my hands over my eyes was of no help, because I needed them to get around. So I used a thick blindfold and shut my eyes. Now the world around me was completely black. I walked around with my hands in front and felt like a child again, playing the game of donkey's tail. Initially, I kept my head down, but then learned that with the head up, I had a better feeling for proportions, for the distances I knew existed between a door and an opposite wall or between pieces of furniture. But even that knowledge wasn't enough. I was still unsure of myself and it wasn't until I placed a blind trust in my hands, a trust that they wouldn't let me walk into something, that I moved with confidence. I quickly learned how many steps there were between the kitchen door and the door of the living room and how long the hallway was. It became a matter of remembering. Of course, the sisters no longer needed to remember. For them it was routine, safely hidden in their subconscious. Walking around with my hands in front to protect myself became easy, but only from the waist up. From the waist down, it was another matter. The arms were of no use for the chairs and low tables that kept standing in the way, unless I walked around bent over at the waist and then I bumped my head against them. The experience made me appreciate even more what Bets and Ann went through, and why, in this house, the pieces of furniture were always standing in the exact same place.

For a week I went around blindfolded all day long, never took the blindfold off, not even at night. As the week progressed I had made two observations that were important to me. I no longer thought of colors and the image of color began to fade. I also felt that within a small world I would be able to function by myself, but that outside, in the big world, I would have to depend entirely on assistance from others. That was the confinement of being blind, as I perceived it from a physical aspect. What my exercise did not teach me was the impact that blindness would have on me as a person. By observing how Bets and Ann had coped with it throughout their lives, I tried to understand that aspect of blindness. They had coped very well. They were two truly happy women. Actually, I considered them happier than most other adult women I had encountered in my life thus far—my mother, my aunts, grandmothers and others. The sisters had amazing inner peace. Of course, they had no immediate family to worry about, to be responsible for, to be hurt by. But on the other hand, they also had not experienced the warmth and love of a husband, of a child, and the giving of love on a

97

personal level other than to each other. Theirs was a smaller world, both physical and emotional.

Caring for, giving and receiving love found its way in our relationships. Bets, very much a down to earth person, could unexpectedly come over and just touch me somewhere. Her hand found my body and moved to where it wanted to touch—a shoulder, a cheek, or, the top of my head. A little tap or two, a smile . . . that was it. It was a motherly way of touching, a fulfillment of a need to express her feeling. And it made me feel good as well. For a long time, she did not like to be touched. She shied away with little motions, like a skittish animal. Only after months, did she enjoy a tap and finally a hug, but it was a hug with a little distance between our bodies. A hug with a quick pulling back, not a lasting one. It went the same way in our conversations. She probed and then responded warmly to what I said, but it took a long time before she opened up and revealed some of her inner feelings.

With Ann, it was quite different. She had a physical presence, liked to touch and be touched. When we sat on the piano stool next to each other and her thigh incidentally touched mine, it did not move away. That would never have happened with Bets. Ann enjoyed a hug, an arm around a shoulder. She was a jovial, more spontaneous person. She expressed herself firmly, self-assuredly. Ann was fun to be with, whereas I felt like protecting Bets.

7

The Toothache

During my third month on Rembrandt Avenue, I developed a toothache in the right upper wisdom tooth. It wasn't too bad the first couple of days, and I hoped that it would go away with some extra brushing, but it didn't. It became worse. I could wiggle the tooth a little bit between my thumb and index finger, which increased the pain, but in a perverse way, I didn't mind. At least it was a change from the constant gnawing pain. The sisters seemed to sense that something was wrong.

"What is the matter?" Ann said during dinner. "You're so quiet."

She was right. I wasn't talking. I was busy swishing saliva around the tooth. "Oh, nothing."

"Yes there is. Something is wrong. What is it?" she insisted.

"Just a little toothache. It'll go away."

I didn't want them to worry and Ann didn't pursue it. The pain persisted and became agonizing. That night, when I looked in the mirror, I noticed that my face was swollen. It also felt warm to my hand.

"How do you feel Barth?" Bets asked the next morning, after Ann had left for the Institute.

"Not too bad."

Bets wasn't satisfied. She came over to where I was sitting and took my face between her hands.

99

"Your face is swollen," she said, alarmed. "We have to do something."

"Yes, but what?"

"You should see a dentist."

"Bets, I don't know any dentist nearby and I can't just go on the street looking for one."

The sisters had a telephone, but they had no use for a regular telephone book. They had memorized a few numbers and the others were all in Braille. Their dentist lived in Amsterdam. I became slightly irritated. It wasn't her fault that I had a sore tooth. It was just that for the first time, I felt lost as to what to do.

"Maybe Ann has an idea. We'll ask her when she comes home."

Poor Bets, she was so concerned, so helpless. Now it was her predicament too. When Ann came home, she didn't hesitate a minute. She felt the warm swelling on the side of my face and right there and then decided what to do.

"You have to see a dentist."

She left no room for argument. She went to the telephone in the hallway and called Mr. Loopstra next door. We could hear her side of the conversation through the open door.

"Mr. Loopstra, this is Annie Frank. Do you know where I can find a dentist nearby?" There was a pause. "Oh, thank you. Thank you very much. Good night."

"There is one around the corner on Nassau Avenue, eight houses down," she said when she came back into the room.

It was winter and dark early. Curfew started at eight o'clock and at nine I left the house and walked around the corner to Nassau Avenue, hugging the garden fences and looking around constantly to make sure that nobody was coming. The danger of being caught didn't come from the Germans. Other than during an organized raid, they were rarely seen in the suburbs. They stayed downtown where the entertainment was. The real danger lay with the ambitious Dutch Nazis and the eager young policemen. Especially after curfew, they were apt to stop me and ask for my papers. Those were the people I had to avoid. There was a black-out after dark and bicycle lamps let only a quarter inch slit of light through, which wasn't nearly enough for a biker to see where he was going, but enough to see someone coming from the opposite side and thus avoid a collision. The darkness was my friend. I saw a bike coming and ducked into a garden. A uniformed policeman passed by and I waited until he turned the corner of Rembrandt Avenue.

It was the ninth house down. There was a white enamel sign with black letters on the side of the house. "Dentist. Office hours 9:00 to 5:00. By Appointment Only.' I rang the bell and after what seemed like a long wait, a small window in the front door opened and a man's voice said, "Yes?"

"Doctor, I have to see you."

"Do you realize that it is after nine o'clock? You have to make an appointment."

"Yes sir, I know it's late, but I can't wait."

"Well, I can't help you without an appointment. Call me tomorrow."

He closed the little window and left me standing on the steps. I rang again. Nothing happened. I rang and kept my finger on the bell. The little window opened and the faceless voice, now irritated, spoke. "Go away."

"I won't. You have to help me now, please."

"I'll call the police if you don't go away."

It didn't sound very convincing. The man was obviously scared. He must have realized that I was no ordinary patient, coming so late in the evening, and he seemed to hesitate behind that little window. At least he didn't close it. I was desperate.

"Doctor, you know that I can't see you during the day-time. It has to be tonight. I wouldn't be here if it weren't really necessary. Please."

101

The little window closed. He opened the door just far enough for me to slip through and led me to his treatment room, where he pointed to an uncomfortable looking dental chair. "Sit down. Let me have a look."

He knew immediately what was wrong.

"You have an infected tooth. I can't do anything while it is infected."

The dentist was middle-aged. He wore a pince-nez on a thin, pointed nose. He was nervous and I had the feeling that he was relieved that he couldn't do anything with the infected tooth.

"Sir, you have to take it out," I said.

"I can't, don't you see? The infection has to calm down first."

"No I don't see. Why do you think I came here at nine o'clock at night? It has to be right now, because I can't take another chance. You have to do something. That tooth has to come out."

He thought for a moment and appeared to be wavering.

"I'm not supposed to do this. You've put my family in danger. Somebody may have seen you."

"Nobody saw me. Now please, pull it out."

"You realize that there is no time to wait for anesthesia to work?"

"I don't care. Just do it."

I was not being a hero, but there wasn't anything I could do under the circumstances. I had no choice. The longer I was there, the more we both were in danger. He was good. He yanked that tooth out in no time and stuffed a big wad of gauze in the wound.

"Bite hard on that for a couple of hours."

For the first time, he sounded sympathetic. He led me back to the front door.

"Wait here."

He went outside and looked around.

"OK, the coast is clear," he said when he came back.

He opened the door once more just far enough for me to slip through and gave me a little pat on the back.

"Good luck."

I mumbled a "thank you" through clenched teeth and found my way back home, where the sisters were anxiously waiting. They wanted to know how it went, but all I could do was point at my jaw and wince, which was stupid of me because they couldn't see the pointing and wincing. They stood facing me, unhappy, not knowing what to do, except to feel sorry for me. And at that moment I felt intensely sorry for them. They looked so vulnerable. I put my arms around their shoulders and walked them back to the living room. I didn't sleep well. In the middle of the night, Ann came into my room.

"Are you asleep?"

"Uh—uh."

"Do you want anything?"

"Uh—uh."

"Try to get some sleep."

She brushed my head with a searching hand, then left. The next morning the throbbing pain was much less and the swelling was gone the day after. I had been very lucky indeed.

8

The Food Shortage

Food became a problem. For many centuries, the waters of the Rhine and the Meuse delta had overflowed their borders and had covered the land with a thick layer of rich silt that formed the essential nutrients for a good crop. Holland, which for a large part consists of the delta of these two rivers, produced plenty of food for its own people and always had a large export. However, that was before the war. Soon after the occupation, the export became massive, all in one direction—East to Germany. Our German 'friends' confiscated or stole anything they could lay their hands on. 'Für das Vaterland,' they said.

"Do you have any idea how much the Germans are stealing from us?" I said one day after dinner.

"Well, we know that there is less to eat," Ann said. "Is that what you mean?"

"It's much more than that. For instance, in two weeks alone, between June 1 and 15, in less than one month after they invaded us, they took 810 tons of cotton, 372 tons of wool, 118 tons of kapok, 9,000 tons of rice, 8,360 tons of grain, 4,430 tons of flour and 1,210 tons of hides."

"What's a ton?" Bets asked.

"A thousand kilos."

"Wow, that's a lot. And it isn't only food."

"It's everything. Do you remember that I told you

about that man IJzerdraat, the one who wrote the first underground paper?"

"Yes we do," Ann said.

"Well, he predicted that we would have rationing. But only for us. The Nazis and the black market racketeers aren't hungry. They can get anything they want."

"We have to thank Seyss-Inquart for this," Bets said.

"True, but from what I have read in the underground press, he himself seems to be an exception in more than one way. He has given his cook, Franz Riesch, strict orders not to obtain anything from the black market. Every month Riesch collects the food coupons from the staff members of 'Clingendael', a countryseat near The Hague, where Seyss-Inquart resides with his beloved wife, Gertrude. Riesch then buys food in the shops nearby. The help eats the exact same food as that served to the master. And he drinks one glass of wine at the most. The story goes that when high-ranking Nazis are invited for dinner, they have their drinks elsewhere, both before and after dinner. Seyss-Inquart wants to have nothing to do with these excesses. If Germans do themselves well with the food and drink stolen from the Dutch, that is their business. He doesn't tolerate it under his roof. Gertrude is different. She was deeply disappointed that Göring refused to visit them at Clingendeal when he toured Holland. Fat Göring had been forewarned about the kitchen at Clingendael."

"I didn't know that Göring is fat," Bets said.

"Are you kidding? He must measure more around his waist than he is tall."

"You said something about Clingendael. Is that a palace?" Ann asked.

"No it isn't, and in that Seys-Inquart is also an exception. He could have taken one of Queen Wilhelmina's palaces, but he wisely didn't consider it. That would really have upset the Dutch."

105

"You said that he was different in more ways than one," Bets said. " What other way?" And different from who?"

"On the one hand he is a devout national-socialist and a trusted follower of Hitler. He betrayed his own country, Austria, and is in large part responsible for the conditions we live in now. On the other hand, he seems to be a modest man and he loves music and opera. Holland could have had a Heinrich, that infamous butcher."

Heinrich, the right-hand man of Himmler, was considered the cruelest of all Gestapo and even the sisters knew about him.

Once a month Dutch families collected their food coupons at a distribution office. One of the students picked them up for the Franks. Of course there were no coupons for me, at least during the first couple of months. Then, one night, Ann heard a slight noise.

"Something fell."

"I didn't hear anything. Did you, Bets?" I said.

"No." She lifted her head and listened. "No, nothing."

"Well, I heard something in the hallway."

Ann, convinced that her superb hearing hadn't fooled her, left the room and triumphantly returned with a thin package.

"See! It was under the mail slot."

We sat around the table, all three of us curious as to what it could be. Bets and Ann took turns examining the thin package and then gave it to me.

"It's wrapped in light brown paper and it has no address."

"Open it." Bets could no longer wait.

"Food coupons. Sheets of food coupons," I cried out.

"How did that get here? Where did it come from?" Ann wanted to know.

There were no answers, only a sober realization. Somebody knew that the sisters had an extra mouth to feed and that somebody had provided. From then on, once a month, a thin package dropped through the mail slot in the front door of the house of the ladies Frank. Always after dark. We didn't learn where it came from or who delivered it until after the war. We were also fortunate that some students lived on farms and, during the later stages of the war, they paid for their lessons with eggs, potatoes and meat. Overall, our situation wasn't really that bad, but the sisters were curious how other people coped with the food shortage, how my family coped.

"Barth, how do your parents make out with this food shortage?" Ann asked one Sunday during lunch. I told them how my family tried to cope.

Near the end of the first year of the war, Mother developed rheumatism and she gradually lost weight. She had been 140 pounds before the war, but now she was a mere 85 pounds. She saw the Dutch Nazi doctor responsible for issuing extra food coupons for the needy, but he declared her healthy enough and refused to give her any. So Dad went to see him. He had been skinny all his life, never above 140 pounds, and he had lost only one or two pounds in weight. One look at him and the same doctor, hearing that Dad worked in heavy construction, issued him double rations for the rest of the war.

We also had a dog, a shorthaired German shepherd with a long pedigree and an even longer official name. We had baptized him "the Baron" and Dad loved that dog. But big dogs needed to eat as well, and beginning in 1942, our third year into the war, there weren't many scraps left for a dog to eat.

We still had horsemeat, but the single store that sold this meat only opened its doors when the owner had butchered a horse and put up a sign in his window *Tomorrow Open 7:00* the day before. That happened only once or twice month and the way to find out about it was to drive by the store every day. The curfew, which the Germans enforced after eight o'clock at night, lasted until four in the morning. When I still lived at home, I sneaked out of the house a little before

107

that time and usually was first or second in line at the store, waiting in the winter cold. We waited as our feet got colder; stomping on the ground no longer prevented them from becoming numb. We blew in our hands and slapped them on our shoulders, trying to get some blood back into them. Without embarrassment, the shivering people standing in line huddled closely together. We stood two abreast and now and then changed places so that not always the same person was exposed to the ice-cold wind that blew along the line. Being the first in line was no great bargain because I had no place to hide from the wind.

By seven o'clock, the line had become very long and people from half way down the line often went home empty-handed, because the butcher and his assistant couldn't care less how they got rid of the meat, as long as it was fast and they could close shop. Near seven o'clock, my sister Coos and brother Jaap joined me and together we carried away twenty pounds of meat or more. Three pounds for the old couple two houses up, two pounds for the widow down the street and five pounds for Mr. Smale and his little German born wife.

Smale, his face grooved from chronic pain, was an invalid with festering ulceration of the bone in his right leg. Mrs. Smale was a generous, roly-poly woman with a gurgling laugh. She was the sweetest woman on earth and fiercely anti-Nazi. Together they barely managed to exist from the little money social welfare brought in. They too got their clothes from the Salvation Army. They were good people. With the little they had, they still hid three Jewish boys in their house. Mother knew that and I learned of it soon thereafter, when one day I brought the meat and saw a young man jump quickly behind the stairwell when I opened the backdoor.

"You saw him, didn't you?" Mrs. Smale asked.

"Yes I did, but then I didn't."

She smiled. Not only did I see him, but I also knew that

his name was Frans and that we had played against each other a few times in soccer matches between our high schools. Now I knew why Mrs. Smale got five pounds of horse meat and the other couples only two or three.

"We have to do something to feed that dog," Dad said one day. "Otherwise we'll have to let him go."

Letting the Baron go was the last thing Dad wanted to do. But horsemeat was too good for the dog, so mother bought cow and calf brains at her regular butcher. The Baron sniffed at it and refuse to eat the brains. But that lasted only until his hunger got the best of him. Reluctant at first, barely nibbling with his long teeth, he took a couple of bites.

"If that dog had been human, we would have seen an expression of distaste on his face," Mother said.

However, the dog's attitude changed completely after Mother cooked the brains. He liked it—liked it so much, in fact, that Mother also took a bite.

"Not bad," she said. "Not bad at all."

From then on, the Baron shared the brains with the rest of the family. Other people found out about it and the source of brains dried up all too quickly.

"We've got to find something else for that dog," Dad said.

So Dad, a practical man who had grown up on the land, went to the abattoir and asked for intestines. He brought home a big bag full. Mother cleaned them and cooked them in her wash boiler, the only pot large enough to hold them. It smelled awful, a repugnant smell that penetrated every corner of the house. When the intestines were cooked, she divided them into smaller containers and let them cool off. Cold, cooked intestines form a jell-like mass with pieces of gut twisted throughout. The Baron had no trouble with it, maybe because he liked the smell. As the war lasted, meat became a scarce sight on the dinner tables in Holland. All other food

109

was also in short supply and hunger became a permanent visitor in most families. Flour became so scarce that the bakers had to use ground-up tulip bulbs and beets to make bread; gray bread that hung in slimy threads when you pulled it apart. No butter, no cheese. That bread and a large winter carrot made up my lunch, which I ate at school, because, riding back and forth between school and home during intermission took too much energy.

'Hunger makes raw beans taste like sweets' is the translation of a frequently used Dutch proverb, but after a while, even that proverb wasn't used anymore. The Baron ate intestines and didn't lose weight.

"That dog looks great," Dad said. "Look how his coat shines. It's the intestines I tell you. That's what does it. Why don't we try it?"

The taste wasn't all that bad when mother heated the intestines up and the smell was no longer important. From that day on, the Baron shared his meals with us. Proud people never heard of eating intestines. The thought of it—the idea—never came up, and if it did in one or two families, they shuddered. They starved. Throughout the war, Dad found ways to scrounge up food from farmers in Loosdrecht in exchange for a repair job here and there. On the plot of land where once Willem and I had cooked the limestone, he again planted potatoes and grew vegetables, but still no tomatoes. He and his mate Piet borrowed a poorly fed old horse and a wagon and traveled to the rich farms in the eastern provinces of Holland. There too they worked, made a new open fireplace in one farm, repaired a ceiling in another, all in exchange for food, and after two weeks, their wagon was full. Twenty miles from home, the horse dropped dead. They sold the dead horse to a butcher in the nearby town and the two men pulled the wagon the rest of the way. Dad found the extra food. Mother did miracles with it. They were survivors.

9

The Doorbell Rings Twice

Friday night, October 22, 1943 and the rain was pouring. A bad night, even for dogs, but a good one for evading the Germans and the Nazi traitors. They stayed inside on a night like this. Ann was rehearsing for her upcoming recital, Bets was reading a book, and I was translating a music script into Braille. That's when the doorbell rang. It never rang in the evening and it took us completely by surprise. Ann struck a wrong note, Bets sat up even straighter and put a hand to her mouth, and I nearly dropped the typewriter from my lap. Normal people would look at each other and wonder who it could be at this late hour, but we were not normal people— two of us couldn't look. We just sat, hoping that whoever it was would go away. The bell rang again, demanding.

"Don't answer it," Bets said.

But the bell insisted and Ann got up.

"I better see who it is." She left the room.

Bets and I stayed behind, waiting, maybe a bit anxious, but at the same time curious. I grabbed a music book from the piano and suddenly, Bets and I were very busy reading from thick Braille books on our laps. I assumed the same posture I always saw the sisters take—head up and tilted a bit. We heard the voices of a man and of Ann in the hallway and it seemed a long time before the front door closed. Ann came back with a strange woman. She wore a dark blue hat, pulled

58-1100G

deep over her eyes and ears, a thin coat that was ill suited for the winter months, and she carried a small suitcase. Water dripped on the floor.

"This is Mrs. Sterk," Ann said. "She is going to stay with us tonight."

It was a statement of fact. Ann had decided that at the front door. She motioned to where Bets was sitting.

"This is my sister Bets."

Mrs. Sterk nodded, unsure of herself.

"And this is Barth." Ann pointed in the wrong direction, not knowing that I had moved. Mrs. Sterk again nodded and our eyes met.

"Welcome," I said.

She seemed relieved that somebody in the house could see.

"How do you do?" she said in a tired voice.

Ann immediately picked up on the voice.

"You must be very tired. Let me show you where you sleep."

Mrs. Sterk nodded to Bets and as she did, water dripped from her soaking wet hat.

"I'm sorry," she said in a dull voice. "I made your floor all wet."

"Don't worry, I'll take care of it," I said. "You have a good long rest."

She followed Ann, looking so pitiful, so worn out. Bets, who hadn't said a word, turned to me, very much puzzled.

"Who is she and why is she here? Why doesn't Ann tell us what's going on?"

"I think I know, Bets. But let's wait for Ann."

I had recognized Mrs. Sterk when she entered the room. Her name wasn't Sterk; it was Stern, an ironic coincidence because my underground name now was also Stern. I also knew that her son Frans, together with two other young men, was underground with Mr. and Mrs. Smale on 84 Egelantierstraat, two houses up from where my parents lived. When Ann joined us again, she gave no explanation. Instead, all she said was, "Let's go to bed, too," and she said it in a way that brooked no opposition.

That night, while Mrs. Sterk slept in a bed in the attic and I was in my little room, I heard Bets and Ann talking for a long time. At last Ann came in to fetch me. We sat on the big bed. Ann explained.

"Mrs. Sterk is a Jew. She was hiding in another home, but the lady of the house became very nervous and asked Mrs. Sterk to leave. The man who brought her here, asked if she could stay overnight with us while he looked for another place for her."

The thought flashed through my mind that it was no coincidence that the man had chosen this house. Someone out there, or a group of people, knew that the ladies Frank would not hesitate to take yet another person in hiding. I kept the thought to myself.

"Ann, don't tell Mrs. Sterk, but that's not her real name. She has taken another name, just like I did. I know who she really is," I said.

"How do you know her," Bets asked.

"Oh, let's just say that I know."

I didn't want to be more specific. Even in this house, the less said about something like that, the better.

"Well," Ann said. "What do you think about letting her stay here with us?"

"She can sleep on the attic and help in the house," Bets added.

"It's fine with me," I said. "But you must realize what you're doing. Hiding a student like me is one thing, but hiding a Jew is quite another matter. When per chance there is a raid, I at least can masquerade as a blind person. There is nothing unusual about that since both of you are blind. And I

113

have some papers to prove it. She has nothing and the Nazis are much tougher with someone who hides Jews. If they ever find her, you may be in real danger."

"Well, as far as we are concerned, we just took in another housekeeper," Bets said.

"No Bets, that's not enough. You can't take it so lightly. I want to be sure that you and Ann know how dangerous this may be. If they catch you, you could end up in jail or worse. Already more than a thousand people, including women, have been sent to concentration camps for helping Jews. And the Nazis are getting tougher every day. You heard what Göring said about us, didn't you?"

"No, we never heard Göring say anything," said Bets.

"He said that of all the nations the Germans have conquered, the Dutch are the most hostile. That's why they try to keep us under such tight control."

The sisters remained silent for a moment, thinking.

"Mrs. Sterk needs help," Ann said after a while. "Other people give it too and for us this is the only way we can help our country."

"Blind people are also part of society," Bets said. "Blindness should not be an excuse. I have a strong feeling about this. We both feel happy doing it."

"And I love you both. You make me very proud to be with you."

"What about food?" Ann wondered. "We'll have another mouth to feed."

The matter was settled and it was time to be practical. I also had thought about that and didn't think we had to worry.

"I have a feeling that if she stays with us, the man who brought her here will come up with something."

The decision was made. It was the right thing to do. The next morning, when Bets told Mrs. Sterk that she could stay, she seemed puzzled.

———

"You mean I can stay with you until they find another house for me?"

"No, you can stay as long as you like. You can live with us." Mrs. Sterk burst out in tears and it took a while for her to compose herself.

"But how does that work with you both being blind?" She wiped the tears away.

"We will manage. You'll see," said Bets, a fine smile on her face. She had heard similar questions before.

Mrs. Sterk looked at me, unsure.

"It'll work out fine. We'll help you, don't worry," I said.

"Thank you," she said, still hesitant, unbelieving.

That night the doorbell rang again. Mrs. Sterk disappeared to the attic and Ann went to open the front door. She came back into the living room with a man.

"This is the gentleman who brought Mrs. Sterk," she said.

The man nodded and did not introduce himself.

"We have decided that Mrs. Sterk can stay with us," Ann said.

"Yes, we'd like to keep her here if that's all right with you" Bets added.

The man smiled.

"I had hoped you would say that. I'll arrange for extra food coupons. Is there anything else you can think of?"

"No. We have everything that a woman will need," Ann laughed. "A man is a different story."

The man looked at me and I looked back, my eyes fixed on his left ear.

"I better be going," he said.

Ann let him out. I called upstairs to Mrs. Sterk that she could come down.

"Is this the second house you'll be in?" Bets asked her.

"No, the fourth."

"The fourth! Why?"

"Well, the first house was much too small. They had a

115

large family and there really wasn't any room for me. But they were very nice people and they let me stay until a new house was found. In the second house there was a problem. After only one month, the husband began to make advances to me and I had to go. And you already know that the lady of the last house had become nervous."

"How about your own family?" I said.

"I hope that they are safe, but I don't know where they are," she said.

"How many in your family?" Ann asked.

"My husband, my son, who is nineteen and my daughter. She is sixteen."

"They'll all be safe. Don't worry," Bets said.

She leaned over and touched her on her arm. Mrs. Sterk brushed a few tears away. She had worried ever since the Germans crossed our borders. She had known no rest. And now, this strange house with two blind women and a young man, who, for one reason or another, lived with them. She needed some time to figure it all out.

And now we were four.

Mrs. Sterk was a healthy, strong woman. A bit on the heavy side and full bosomed. I noticed. She had a handsome face and her smile revealed a space between her upper front teeth. Despite the fact that her entire family was dispersed and that she didn't even know where they were or whether they were still alive, she maintained a remarkably positive outlook on life. When she came downstairs in the morning, her "Good morning" and smile radiated a certain happiness. She was a pleasant woman, always ready to help, and with her in the house it was no longer necessary for a cleaning lady to come in.

"You are also hiding, aren't you?" she said, when, in the afternoon of her third day with us, we were alone in the living room. "And your real name isn't Stern, is it? Such a Jewish name."

I looked her in the eyes and didn't answer. She turned away.

"Sorry, I shouldn't have asked."

"It's all right. Let it rest."

There was a major problem to be solved. Mrs. Sterk could not masquerade as a blind person. Her strong Jewish facial features were a dead give-away and, most importantly, she had no papers.

"We have to find a good hiding place for you just in case there is a razzia," I said.

"What's a razzia?" asked Bets.

"That's when the Germans close off part of the town and do a house to house search for Jews and people like me."

The question was where?

"Behind the stairs in the cellar," Ann suggested, but I rejected it.

"That'll be one of the first places they look."

"I know! We can hide you on the attic. They won't go there," Bets said.

This was one of few occasions in which the sisters in their blindness did not appreciate, could not visualize, how a seeing person would immediately discover those two obvious places. Of course Germans looking for Jews or men without an Ausweis would go to the attic. I suggested that we go look for a suitable place.

"It has to be a space so small that a German wouldn't even bother to look for it. Why don't we make a tour of the house and look for places like that."

"Good idea," said Ann.

As if by instinct, we started a procession with the upstairs. I was in front, followed by Ann, then Bets and Mrs. Sterk brought up the rear. We looked in every room, in all closets and each corner, but found nothing to our liking. Our little procession next took the stairs to the attic. In essence, this was a large, empty space. Mrs. Sterk's bed stood in a

117

corner, with a chair and a chest of drawers containing her few clothes. We had already considered that this would not be unusual if anybody asked about the clothes, because along the walls were several closets and drawers with the clothes of Bets and Ann, stored there for the season.

"How about under the dormer window?" Mrs. Sterk asked.

"That may not be such a bad idea," I said.

"Where?" The sisters said in chorus.

Mrs. Sterk took first Bets, then Ann by the hand and let them touch the three walls of the dormer. They knocked on each wall and it was obvious from the hollow sound that there was space behind them.

"That's it."

Immediately they were enthusiastic, but after thinking about it for a while, I also rejected that idea.

"Just think about it for a moment. How is she going to get in there? It means that we'll have to cut out an opening in the wall and then make an invisible door. I don't think it'll work, because they'll see that the wall has been tampered with." "Can't we hang something over it?" Bets asked.

"No. They'll look behind it."

Downstairs we went and back to the bedrooms.

"A closet. We can make a hiding place in a closet." From my years of working with my Dad, I knew that the ceilings of most closets were lower than the ceiling of the adjacent room. That meant that there could be a space between the ceiling of the closet and floor of the room above it, large enough to hide a person. And we didn't have to make a door. I explained it to the others and the enthusiasm returned, but the sisters had some reservations.

"How can Mrs. Sterk climb up there?"

"What are you going to do with the ceiling of the closet?"

"What is it made of?"

"Will it be large enough?"

Their questions came in rapid fire, the answers more slowly. In the end, we decided to give it a try. Thank goodness old Mr. Frank had long ago decided that his daughters would need their own tools for him to work with when he came over to repair something. The ceiling in the closet was made of wood and I was ready with the saw under close supervision of the three ladies.

"Shouldn't you measure it first?" Ann said.

"Good idea." Bets added.

The ceiling measured forty-eight inches wide and eighteen inches deep.

"How about Mrs. Sterk? Can she fit?" Bets said.

Mrs. Sterk stood with her back to the wall and I measured her to be nineteen inches, front to back. It wouldn't work. Ann didn't buy it.

"Nineteen inches?" she said, amazed.

"Yes, nineteen inches, and the closet is eighteen."

Ann moved over to Mrs. Sterk and felt her breasts.

"They are big."

"What are big?" Bets said.

"Her breasts."

"Let me feel."

Bets felt and Mrs. Sterk blushed deeper and deeper.

"You can push them in." Bets pressed on the voluptuous breasts. "Here, Barth, you do it and then measure her."

"Oh, no. Not me."

Now it was my turn to blush. I wasn't going to touch those breasts. No way. The women burst out in laughter.

"I'll press and you measure." Mrs. Sterk giggled.

I put the end of the measuring staff against the wall and eyed the front of the breasts.

"Seventeen and a half inch."

"We did it," the sisters exclaimed triumphantly.

I carefully cut out the ceiling along the edges and, with screws, attached two feet long planks across the width of the

119

cutout ceiling, on the top, so that the ceiling hung freely in its place when it was closed. Mrs. Sterk would have to sit or lie on top of it once she was in the space. We were ready to give it a try. I put a chair in the closet, Mrs. Sterk climbed up, removed the false ceiling, and handed it to me.

"Up you go," I said and up she went, arms and head first.

But Mrs. Sterk was no athlete. She wriggled her breasts passed the opening, shoved herself in further and then came to an abrupt halt. We had forgotten something.

"I'm stuck." The voice in the crawl space was muffled.

"What's happening?" the sisters wanted to know.

"She is stuck."

"Did she press her breasts in?"

"It's not her breasts. It's her behind."

"Oh."

"What are you saying?" Mrs. Sterk said in a muffled voice.

"Nothing."

"What?"

"You're stuck." I raised my voice.

"You're telling me."

Bets climbed on the chair and felt around Mrs. Sterk's behind.

"She is fat." Bets never minced words.

"Come back," I said.

Mrs. Sterk wriggled and twisted. Her heavy legs flapped and she didn't move an inch.

"I can't push off. Get me out of here." Her muffled voice became frantic.

"We'll pull you out."

I tried to get a hold of her legs, but she was still kicking.

"Stop kicking."

"What?"

"Hold still." This time Ann raised her voice.

We each grabbed a leg and pulled hard. Mrs. Sterk shot loose like a cork from a champagne bottle and plopped on top of us so that all three of us landed on the floor. The poor woman's face was red as a beet. For a moment, it looked like she would cry, but then, as she saw us sprawled on the floor, she started to laugh. Ann and I also laughed.

"What happened? Why are you on the floor?" Bets wanted to know.

"Mrs. Sterk fell on top of us and we all dropped down," I said.

"Well get up."

"Don't you think that's funny?" Ann said.

"No." Bets couldn't see it.

"What'll we do now?" Ann said.

"We're going to look for another place."

"But what about the hole in the closet?" Mrs. Sterk said.

"We will put the false ceiling back in place and leave it as it is," I said. "If the Germans ever raid this house and insist on looking around and find it, there'll be nothing there and you can say that at one time your nephew made it for himself. That'll satisfy them."

"Where do we go next?" Bets was in the mood of the moment.

We looked at every room downstairs and couldn't come up with a solution. As we stood in the hallway thinking about it, Bets suddenly came up with an idea.

"We can make a hiding place right here, right where we're standing."

"You mean under the floor?" Ann asked her.

"Yes. When people come through the front door into the hallway, they'll be standing right on top of it. They'll never think of looking down there."

Mrs. Sterk and I looked at each other.

"What do you think?" she asked.

"Well, it may just work. Bets, Ann, do you know that this hallway has a beautiful parquet floor? I'll have to cut out a piece and it'll never be the same again."

121

"What is a parquet floor?" Ann said.

Mrs. Sterk explained.

Bets pouted. "It's just a floor. Who cares?"

Ordinary people would care, but why should she? She had never seen the floor and didn't know the difference from other floors. Ann put her two cents in.

"All the more reason for them not to look there. We will put a rug over it and nobody will know."

The sisters had already made up their minds. I cut a two-foot square opening in the floor of the hallway, directly behind the door of the pass-through. Stale air met us. There was a foot deep crawl space under most of the house and all I had to do was enlarge an area so that Mrs. Sterk would be comfortable. The extra sand was dispersed under the rest of the house and I fixed strong slats along all sides of the hole so that they formed a one-inch resting-place for the cover, which I made of the original wood. We were once again ready to try it out. This time, Mrs. Sterk had no trouble getting in and when the thick hallway rug was pulled back in place, it was impossible to tell that there was a hiding place underneath it.

Next we had to decide what each of us would do during a raid.

"I'll open a window in our bedroom to tell them that we are blind and ask them to wait a while," Bets said.

Ann volunteered to pull the rug aside and open the hiding place. I was the youngest and the fastest and therefore would do the running up and down the stairs. All Mrs. Sterk had to do was to get into the crawl space with some of her belongings. We were all set for our first rehearsal. Ann woke me up in the middle of the night. I ran upstairs to wake Mrs. Sterk, grabbed her pillow and sheets while she collected her few clothes and toilet articles, and down we ran two flights of stairs to the hallway. Bets opened an upstairs window to stall the Germans, or whoever would be at the door. Ann pulled the rug back and opened the hole for Mrs. Sterk to slide into. I then covered the hole, put the rug back in place, and sneaked back upstairs to my room. Only then did Ann open the door. All this was done in complete darkness because all three occupants were supposed to be blind and didn't need light. That first time was a disaster. I had trouble waking Mrs. Sterk, who turned out to be a sound sleeper. Later, I learned to give her a good slap in the face for immediate results. Ann pulled the heavy rug in the wrong direction so that we stumbled over it when we came racing down the stairs, and Bets completely forgot her lines. Also, we treated the rehearsal as if it were a big joke. We made too much noise and the whole exercise lasted about five minutes, which was much too long. Last but not least, when Mrs. Sterk climbed out of the hiding place, she was covered with sand. We put an old blanket on the bottom of the hole and we rehearsed again and again, night after night, until we finally had the timing down to less than a minute and hardly made any noise. From then on, Ann set her alarm clock at odd hours once every two or three weeks for a surprise rehearsal. All this time, the two sisters regarded it as great fun, something new and exciting in their lives, especially Bets. She clapped her hands together and said, "I feel like I'm part of the real world." The hideout became known as 'The Hole.'

"Did you hear Ann say see to Bets?" Mrs. Sterk asked the next morning.

"Yes I did."

"Don't you think that strange, coming from her?"

"Not really. You'll get used to it. We say it all the time."

"Hmm. Amazing."

Then came the night that it was not a rehearsal. A strange sound outside awakened Bets and Ann, both light sleepers. Ann came in my room and woke me up.

"Barth, something going on outside. Listen to that sound. What is it?"

123

I listened and then heard it too—a faint rustling sound. I pulled the curtain aside and saw them. At four o'clock in the morning, there were columns of German soldiers walking by on their socks, their boots dangling from their shoulders. Hundreds and hundreds shuffled along, out of step, almost noiseless so as not to wake the citizens. They came from Nassau Avenue, around the corner of the Loopstra house, passed our house and turned left into Vermeer Avenue, which ran along the school. I had no idea what it was all about, but it certainly didn't look good.

"Germans, hundreds of them. There's going to be a razzia somewhere."

"Why don't we hear them?"

"They're not wearing their boots."

"They must be up to something."

"I don't like it. We better put Mrs. Sterk in the hole."

Without realizing we had been whispering. Ann returned to her bedroom to tell Bets and I went to the attic to wake Mrs. Sterk, who was snoring as usual. Waking her again required a slap on her cheek. Without a word, she jumped out of bed, grabbed her few belongings and started to run for the stairs, just like she did during the rehearsals. I stopped her.

"Mrs. Sterk, it's not a rehearsal. It's just a precaution."

I quickly explained what was going on outside and then, still not saying a word, she proceeded downstairs, where Ann was already waiting at the hole. But before she went in, Bets gave her a hug.

"It's nothing. You'll see," she said.

In the darkness I couldn't see Mrs. Sterk's face, but I felt the fear. This time it wasn't much fun. The seriousness of our situation grabbed us and we were all strangely quiet.

Two days later, we learned from a student that there had been a massive raid in the nearby Tree Quarter of town. When the people in that neighborhood woke up in the morning, they found a soldier, rifle in hand, standing in front of their

house and one in the back on top of the bicycle shed. No one
was allowed outside until the soldiers had searched every
house from top to bottom. They were looking for Jews and
able-bodied men below age fifty.

Mrs. Sterk was in the "hole" for more than an hour during the night the Germans walked passed our house and we
discussed what would happen if she needed to hide for a
longer time.

"I would like to have some water handy," she said.

"What if you have to go to the bathroom?" asked Bets.

"Well, it's just sand down there." I was thinking what a
man would do.

"No, we'll give you a bucket," said Ann.

"Is there anything else you can think of Mrs. Sterk?" I
asked.

"Did you hear me cough?" she asked.

"No we didn't."

"She needs cough drops," said the ever practical Bets.

"Were you comfortable down there," Ann asked.

"I could have used a pillow, because my neck got stiff."

And so we stored a bucket, a bottle with water, cough
drops and a pillow in the "hole" for future use, which we all
hoped, would never be needed. Mrs. Sterk and I also needed
to take extra precautions. We reminded ourselves constantly
not to stand too close to the large front window, especially
on Fridays when the sisters were in Amsterdam. The sisters
were well-known in town and if people familiar with their
routine happen to pass by and notice a figure in the house,
they might alert the police. Also on those days I didn't dare
play an instrument, again because a passerby might hear it
while knowing that the sisters were not at home. Those were
the most boring days for me. And since they came back late
from Amsterdam, Mrs. Sterk and I had to wait in darkness for
their return. Even with the curtains tightly drawn some faint
light might be visible from the street.

Razzias continued throughout the occupation, but especially during the last twelve months, when the German war machine became desperately short in slave labor. The largest razia in Hilversum took place on October 23-24, 1944, when the Germans arrested 3761 men. Of these 819 were forced to make tank barricades around Arnhem. The rest were shipped to Germany, where they were put to work near Osnabruck. Those who escaped this razzia went underground, including Casper Baas and Adriaan Kuijsten, who found a most unusual shelter. What better place they thought than the lion's den? The father of Casper was responsible for the technical maintenance of the town hall even while this was the headquarters of the German army. The friends and two others brazenly walked passed the German guard at the door and were met by Mr. Baas, who hid them in the space between the ceiling of the council hall and the roof. There they stayed, while below the German high command held meetings.

10

Thoughts

Being cooped up inside month after month sometimes got the best of me. I tried to keep busy with my studies on the piano, flute and cello, with translating a book or music score into Braille, and by doing a few physical exercises, which I found boring. But in the long run, all that wasn't enough. There were no books to read and no games to play, other than chess with Ann. The pieces had a peg at the bottom, which fitted into holes in the center of each square. The black pieces had a pointed top, the white tops were rounded. The board was eight inches square and using two hands Ann could feel the entire board. After a few months I started playing blindfolded.

I had lots of time to just sit and think. All three women in our house were at least twice my age. They were nice, but I had no physical interest in them. I was nineteen and had little or no experience with women. One time, when I was fourteen, a girl in our street and I went canoeing and she had let me touch her left breast. That was the closest I had ever been with a girl and I remembered how firm and perfectly round that breast had been—smooth as marble when my hand went around the curves. I now wondered about its beauty, but it didn't arouse me. It was too far away.

I thought about Nienke, the girl I had never touched or kissed. The girl I was in love with, the one who was unreachable.

127

It had been a cold afternoon in January 1939 that I first saw her. The ice lay thick on the canals and even the plassen of Loosdrecht were solidly frozen. I was sitting on the grass on the side of the canal putting on my skates and there she was, some fifty feet away. She wore a yellow sweater embroidered with red flowers and green leaves, a yellow bonnet, and yellow mittens. A young man kneeled before her and tied the laces of her skates. I was fifteen and instantly in love. Eight months later, when high school resumed after the summer vacation, she came through the classroom door and looked around, squinting. She walked to an empty seat in the fourth row from the door, second seat from the front. The new teacher began a roll call with Adama, Catharina.

"Nienke, my name is Nienke," she said in a firm, precise voice.

Nienke Adama. She must be Friesian. I thought. Nearly all people from Friesland had a name that ended with an "a." Every day she rode her bicycle to school with her friends, laughing and talking, and I wasn't part of her world. She lived in a well-to-do neighborhood, in one of the villas my Dad had built for Mr. Bloemenkamp, the villas I had worked in. Across the street from her house was a large decorative pond. After dark, sure that I couldn't be seen, I drove slowly by her house and when I saw her studying, her head bent under the lamp, I stood at the other side of the pond, loving her from afar.

She did poorly in math and physics, but she tried. She tried so hard that one day she bit her lip and a drop of blood fell on her paper. I noticed. She came close to tears when Mr. van Dop, the math teacher, sometimes became too sarcastic. But she didn't cry and I was proud of her. On the hockey field across the school, she ran with the other girls of our class, ungainly with long legs and arms, already mature breasts bouncing up and down. I watched her blowing a hair from her nose, wiping the sweat from her brow with the back of her hand. So healthy, so beautiful, so far.

During our last school year, we sat again in the same class, together with three German sympathizers, members of the Nazi Youth movement. Their leader was Jan de Wijn, a stocky fellow with a crew cut. The other fellow, Han Wolters, had red hair like mine. He was a wimpy boy who followed de Wijn everywhere. The girl, Greet Loohuis, wasn't that bad. Her parents were Nazis and she seemed embarrassed by it. On January 31, 1942, the birthday of Princess Beatrix, de Wijn and Wolters showed up in their Nazi Youth uniform, ready to make trouble. Tinie Veenstra, another Friesian, lived out of town and she always brought a bottle of orange juice for lunch and, as she did every day, she had put the bottle on the windowsill next to her. Mr. Rutgers, our director, taught astronomy the first hour. For the second hour we had a substitute teacher and that's when de Wijn made his move.

"I want that bottle removed, right now." He pointed to it.

During the German occupation, any reference to the royal family was strictly forbidden and orange was the color of the House of Orange. The teacher, an ungainly man with a bald head and egg-shaped face, began to blush. It started in his neck and slowly moved upwards until even his scalp was red. Already a stutterer, he only managed to say, "W—w—why?"

"Goddamn it," de Wijn yelled. "You know damn well why she put that bottle up there. Get it off."

The teacher was sweating. He tried but couldn't say anything. There was dead silence in the class. We were all stunned by the sudden attack and the unheard of language. We waited to see what the teacher would do, but he didn't do anything, just stood there, frozen.

"Is this the best example of what the new master race can do?" I couldn't resist.

Wolters jumped up. "Keep your Goddamn mouth shut."

"Hear, hear, his master's voice," I shot back.

My eye caught Nienke looking at me. She smiled, as if

129

encouraging me. By now, the teacher had regained his composure and he sent de Wijn to the Director's office with his demand. Soon thereafter, Mr. Rutgers came into the class. "Was that bottle standing on the window sill during the first hour?" he said, ever so quietly.

"Yes, sir," a chorus replied.

We could almost sense that Mr. Rutgers knew that he would be in trouble.

"The bottle can stay where it is," he said.

But Mr. Rutgers had become a marked man after that episode. At noontime that Saturday, after the final bell, some of us bigger boys found Mr. Rutgers holding the front door shut. From the other side several Nazis in their black uniforms tried to get in.

"Hold the door while I call the police," Rutgers said.

We held the door, some of us from the inside, others from the outside. There was some pushing and shoving, some yelling and swearing, but it didn't come to a real fight.

"We're getting help," a student who was looking through a side window yelled.

About a dozen workers, armed with pickaxes and shovels, walked from across the street, where they had been clearing a field. They made a half-circle around the Nazis.

"What's going on?" the foreman of the workers asked.

The Nazis looked at each other, looked at the pickaxes. One of them made a motion with his head and they drooped off. The workers stayed until the police arrived.

But that was not the end of it. That same evening Mr. Rutgers was taken hostage by the Germans, together with about forty other notables. After six weeks in prison he was released and returned to school looking like he had lost a lot of weight and never recovered completely from his ordeal. To make his life more miserable, the Nazis appointed a dour faced bald-headed collaborator by the name of van Drie as the new school custodian. The whole atmosphere at school suffered by the mere presence of that man. During the next two months, I was taken out of class twice. The assistant director, Mr. de Waard, the same man who had called me a redhead during the entrance exam, came into our class accompanied by a Nazi in uniform.

"Hoogstraten, pick up your books and papers and follow me," he ordered.

In his office, another Nazi went through my possessions, looking for anything that could be interpreted as being anti-German. On trees or lamp post around town it wasn't unusual to see a drawing of Hitler, hanging from the gallows, or, in large letters, 'Stuff yourself with cork, you German swine, so you'll stay afloat on your way to England.' That was the kind of stuff they were looking for. In the meanwhile, the other Nazi searched my bench and the wall beside it for derogatory remarks. I would have been in deep trouble if they had found anything like that, but Mother had forewarned me and they found nothing.

Sometimes, when Nienke was riding alone, I joined her on the way home or to school. Not as friends, as classmates. When the time came to study for the final National High School Exam, I offered to help her with math and physics, subjects in which she was weak, and she accepted. We worked together for three weeks, upstairs in her mother's bedroom. She sat on one side of the table, I on the other. Three and a half-hours in the morning, four in the afternoon and three in the evening. I went home for meals. We never talked of anything else while we studied. I didn't dare. I didn't want to study on the last Sunday, the day before the exam began, but she insisted on solving one more difficult math problem. We did, and then we walked the heather with her dog Prent. Mrs. Adama had prepared tea when we returned and that's when Mr. Adama spoke of the Friesians, their beautiful black horses, their cows that produced more milk and with a higher fat content than any other cow in the world and of their clean

131

scrubbed farms. The Friesians were proud people who still spoke their centuries old Celtic language that nobody else in Holland could understand. Mr. Adama told a story about a young couple walking after Sunday morning church service on the road below the dike. He on one side of the road, she on the other. Neither said a word. Finally, at long last, he spoke.

"You notice something?"

On they walked. Thirty minutes went by.

"What?" Twenty minutes later.

"I am courting you."

Fifteen minutes of silence.

"I noticed."

Mr. Adama had laughed the loudest about the story. That was the Friesian way. Theirs was a silent love—steady and deep. I now wondered why Mr. Adama told that story that day? The next morning, we assembled in the gym hall where the exam was given. Nienke sat in the next row over, three tables ahead of me. Math came first and the first problem was identical to the one we had solved the day before. She turned around, a happy smile on her face. Nienke scored a nine out of a possible ten in algebra, an eight in math, and a perfect ten in physics. She was always strong in languages and in the end had one of the best final exams of our class.

Her parents gave a party to celebrate and she invited her friends. I also went, not realizing those friends meant girls, and I was a stranger, the only boy there. They laughed and talked loudly. I didn't belong and left. No need to say anything, not good night. A friend of her father came after me at the door and he thanked me. It was the last time that I saw her before going into hiding. Now, thinking about her, as I was in my room alone, I knew that I still loved her.

The one thing I didn't have to think about was that eventually I was going to be a doctor, no matter how impossible that dream now seemed. That had already been decided long ago. But how was I going to get back into medical school after the war? Where would the money come from? The war had impoverished our country and surely there wouldn't be any funds available for my study grant. And how long was this war going to last? The idea of the Germans staying permanently in Holland had never crossed our minds. "After the war" was a given, an absolute certainty. They were going to lose this war, period. It was only a matter of time and this was already the fourth year.

I thought about death and it didn't scare me. I remembered Karel, the boy in the bed next to me in the hospital, the one who had died.

"Are you sick?" he had asked.

"No, I just have to have an operation," I said. "Did you have an operation?"

Karel looked at me, tired looking. "I'm sick. There's something wrong with my blood. I've been here a long time. Are you scared?"

"Nah, I'll be put to sleep."

I was scared all right, but not so that I would let him know. When I woke up from surgery and they brought me back to the ward, Karel asked what the operating room looked like, but I couldn't tell him, because I had been asleep the whole time. He became very weak and one day a priest did something with him that I didn't understand.

"What did that priest do with you?"

"He gave me the last rights," he said.

"What does that mean?"

"They think I'm going to die."

I had to think about that for a while.

"Karel. Are you scared to die?"

"No," he said. "I'll go to heaven."

I still didn't understand, but I was afraid to ask more. He hardly said a word after that and when I woke up one morn-

133

ing, there was a screen around his bed. A nun sat with him all day. A little light was kept on at night and I could see her shadow through the screen. Two days later, the screen was gone and his bed was empty. The nun who made my bed said that he had gone to heaven. Her eyes were red and she kept blowing her nose.

He had gone so quietly, so without fear, so easy. Death wouldn't be so bad if you learned to accept it, I thought. The animals also made no fuss about it, so why should I? In my thinking about dying there was no heaven, no God to make it easier. I had nothing against a God and understood why other people believed in God, why they gained strength from their belief. But in my mind, man had created God, not the other way around. They created many gods, including one who, according to Aztec priests, needed to be appeased by tearing hearts out of people. It took a while before Jesus came and preached of a loving God. And even then, man created a hell. And man began to make war in the name of their God, intolerant as they were when some other group interpreted the same God in a slightly different way. Holland had fought for eighty years because the Spaniards insisted that all Protestants were evil and couldn't go to heaven. Wars. Even German soldiers wore a band around their caps that said 'In God we Trust' when they went into battle killing other people. God was good for everything. 'It was the will of God' people said when hundreds died in an accident or freak of nature. These were my thoughts about religion. I did not need a god. I did not need that make-believe world. I figured that I could just be and let come what would come after death, if anything came. One time I asked Bets what she expected after death. Would she go to the Grail?

"Oh, I don't think so. There are probably several steps on the ladder higher than a human being. Maybe I will go down instead of up." She chuckled.

Bets of all people. So good, so pure, so gentle. In my

book, if angels existed, Bets was going to be one for sure. Being blind all her life and sheltered from a large part of the outside world must have played a big role in her remaining so pure. Many a time I saw her dismiss nastiness, ugliness. With a swing of her left arm she would say, 'That's pure rot,' and that was the end of it.

For a while, Ann tried to get me involved in their religion, but when I read the material she gave me, I couldn't get interested. It was again all make-believe. It seemed to me that her Leader had borrowed most of his ideas from Buddhism and from the ancient cult of metempsychosis, where in a soul could be around for a long time, going from man to animal or plants. But I didn't say that to Bets and Ann, who placed their trust in their cult. As long as they were comfortable with it, who was I to argue with it?

Strangely, my thoughts were without much emotion. It was just thinking, only thinking. The months had dulled the emotion, had replaced it with a certain peace, a restful feeling that could easily be replaced by emptiness. Just sitting and staring, being empty. I didn't feel sorry for myself, just totally empty. After a while, I would take my cello and play the deep, low, beautiful notes. No melody. Gradually, the beauty of the sound replaced the emptiness. I felt it first in my head, then in my chest, a fullness. After a while, there was happiness.

It was around that time that I wrote a few poems. Before the war, Ann had set a poem written by her sister Riek to music. The children's' choir of the AVRO, a leading radio station in Holland, sang it quite often and it became very popular. Children in the street sang it. "Hoor je wel mijn kleppers gaan?" went the first line; "Do you hear the clacking of my castanets?"

Ann put two of my poems to music and sent them in for publication. Music by Annie Frank and text by Ernst Stern, it said. To our surprise, we heard a children's choir sing one of

135

the songs a few months later. "Het Hertje" was the title, "The Little Fawn."

We lived a quiet, uncomplicated, life. Ann went to the Institute, Bets gave lessons, Mrs. Sterk busied herself around the house or spent time in the attic, and I occupied myself as best I could. Once a week, on Friday, the two sisters went to Amsterdam, where they still gave lessons in the music school on Anna Vondel Street, and Mrs. Sterk and I had the house to ourselves. One day she said "I have a son your age," and she talked about him for a while.

"He went to the Gymnasium. He was such a good student."

Oh, how close I came at that moment in telling her that I knew her son and that I knew where he was. It could be too much for her to bear and she might get the urge to go to him. I bit my tongue, because she should not know what I knew. It was one of the unspoken rules during the war: 'Don't tell.' One never knew what could happen. We knew that the Gestapo tortured their prisoners into telling what they knew. But they couldn't tell what they didn't know. To Mrs. Sterk, I was a stranger, as she was to me.

"He loves to play soccer, left forward, because he runs fast and kicks with his left leg."

"I played soccer when I was in the HBS, but I was a goalkeeper. You know we may have played against each other. Did he ever play in the stadium during the inter-school matches?"

"Yes, he did, and his team went to Utrecht for the regional championship." Mrs. Sterk smiled widely at the memory.

"So did our team and in the finals we must have played against him. Does your son also have red hair?"

"He sure does." Now she really laughed.

"Does he also play an instrument?" I asked.

"No, he can't even sing. He likes to, but boy, does he sing false. We once gave him a violin, but that turned out to be a big mistake. Our ears could stand it for only two weeks and then we gave the violin away."

She smiled, and sat quietly, hands in her lap, head down. "He'll be all right; you'll see," I said after an uncomfortable pause.

She got up, ruffled my hair, and went upstairs. Her eyes were red rimmed when she came downstairs later that afternoon. I also went to my room and thought about my years in school and my short time as a medical student.

"He has a photographic memory," Mr. Tijdsma told Mother when he let me skip classes. However, when it was time for me to go to high school, he considered me too young and instead sent me for a year to an intermediary school, the MULO, the same school that was now opposite the Frank's house. But his tutoring had been so good that I didn't learn much that year over what I already knew. I began to read instead, read every book mother brought from the library for herself. During the summer months, I sat in the bedroom window reading by the light of the moon until mother took the book away from me.

"Don't you think its time to go to sleep? You'll ruin your eyes."

She wasn't really scolding. On the day of the admission exam for the HBS, I had my first run in with the assistant director, Mr. de Waard, who supervised the classroom in which we did the exam. I was finished and looked out of the window. "You, with the red hair, look straight ahead," de Waard ordered.

"But I'm finished, sir."

"You can't be finished. Look ahead."

I was angry that he had singled me out by my hair and put the stare on him in the hope that it would make him feel

137

uncomfortable. After a while, he had enough of that and he let me go. High School classes began on August 21. Our first hour was geography with Mr. Vet, a small, frail man, who had been at the HBS since its opening in 1903 and it was to be his last year. The students never took advantage of the little man. They respected him and affectionately called him 'Vetje,' the diminutive of 'Vet.' Sometimes he even introduced himself as 'Vetje.' He maintained order in his class without trying. That first hour he told us to take out our world atlas and, beginning at zero meridian, we identified every country, river, town, lake, volcano, and mountain on the equator. It was a long list and when we finished, Mr. Vet offered a chocolate bar for the first student who could recite the list by heart. That said, he settled down to do some administration.

"I can do that," I said before he could do so.

"You think so?" he said, amazed.

"Yes sir."

"Well, go ahead. Try it."

I got the chocolate. Mr. Vet, now bemused, offered another bar for anybody who could do it backwards. Without pause, I did it. Two chocolate bars. My photographic memory had come in handy and continued to do so until I was about twenty years old, when it began to slow down a bit.

I never needed to study for geography or history. Mr. Sam Preger, our history teacher, taught me a lesson I'll never forget as long as I live. He used to announce his quarterly tests two weeks in advance, saying that the questions would cover a period of about eighty pages in the history book. I read them the night before and the next day knew the answer to each question verbatim by page and paragraph. In between the big exams, he also gave us a chance to get a few extra points that could influence his evaluation for our report cards. Once a month, in the middle of class, he ordered us to close our books and put a scrap of paper and pencil before us. He then gave five short questions, the answers to which were usually dates in history. It was a game my Dad and I had played many times. He gave the date and I gave the answer. He loved it if I had all hundred correct.

In our fourth school year, the boys in Mr. Preger's class had figured out a system to beat the odds. They put a second piece of paper on their knee and when Preger gave the answers, they wrote them down on the second piece. The girls were not in on this. The teacher asked who had five and who had four correct answers. It was an honor system, because he did not always ask for the pieces of paper. In his little book, he gave the students two extra points for five correct answers and one for four. Near the end of the school year, Mr. Preger smelled a rat. One day, he ordered all boys to stay after hours and proceeded to give us fifty short questions. When we were finished, he collected our papers.

"You all know where this is about," he said. "I will grade you on the result of this test, not on the ones we did during the year."

It made me angry.

"Sir, when we had you for the first time four years ago, you said that you would trust us, but if you caught one of us cheating, you would never trust that student again. You didn't catch any of us, so now you're going back on your word."

I turned around and walked away.

"Just a moment," Mr. Preger said. "When you say something like that, you look a man in his eyes and give him a chance to reply. You do not turn your back on him." He took our papers and tore them up. "You'll be graded as if nothing has happened. You can go now." I felt the blood rising from the neck up, a mixture of lingering defiance and deep shame for what I had done. Not for what I had said, but for turning my back before he had a chance to respond. Soon after that episode, the Jew Sam Preger was no longer allowed to teach by the Germans.

Our best teacher by far and the one I respected most,

was Mr. Arie Van Dop, the math teacher. He was strongly built, had thinning black hair, wore dark rimmed glasses and he smoked cigars. He had a tremendous sense of humor and wore the suggestion of a smile on his face. He was, above all, a Christian. If I had to guess, religion came first in his life, teaching second, and family third. He was a stern disciplinarian who could bring tears in the eyes of the girls and put a scare in the boys. However, because no teacher worked harder than he did, he had the respect of every pupil in his classes and there was never a need for him to discipline a student. When occasionally a boy dared to give a rash reply to a question, van Dop just looked at him with a smile and said, "Java Lane 4." That was all, Java Lane 4. His house on Java Lane 4 was famous throughout town among high school students. The boy better show up. During each quarter, he gave three tests, which usually consisted of solving four problems, which he wrote out on the blackboard that day. At the end of the hour, he collected the papers and graded them at home. During the first semester I solved the problems well before the hour was over and handed my paper in. "You have a ten," he announced each time.

When students did poorly on tests on more than one occasion, van Dop went all out to help them. "Java Lane 4," was the verdict. It was quite normal for him to have a dozen pupils in various rooms at the same time, two or three in a room, including the bedrooms. Only his living room was sacrosanct. The pupils were given a few problems to solve and if they were not ready after an hour or so, he helped them out. In addition he gave private lessons to students from other schools. I was in his house twice during my five years at the HBS. The first time came during the second semester of the first year. On two consecutive tests he announced "A six," and he looked at me. I knew I had solved the problems correctly and I was stunned. "Java Lane 4," he said after the second six and I went. Mrs. Van Dop opened the door.

"You can go right upstairs," she said.

Mr. van Dop handed me a piece of paper and escorted me to a small bedroom. I shared a table with another first year student, a girl, who had a difficult time with a problem. She tried so hard, tears welled in her eyes, but she couldn't find the answer. Reading upside down, I knew the answer to the problem and indicated that she should lengthen the baseline of the triangle. She went on to solve the problem. Van Dop had given me two problems to solve and when I handed them in he said, "Don't be in such a hurry to hand in your paper in class. You obviously know how to solve the problems, but then you make the slightest mistake and come out with the wrong answer. Take your time to look it over before you hand them in."

I thanked him and left, but not before he dryly added, "By the way, she would never have found the answer if you hadn't helped her." He smiled.

From then on, I had tens again. During the last month before graduation, van Dop always gave his class five problems to solve over the weekend. However, unlike in other tests, these problems were so difficult that he didn't expect them to be solved.

"You do well if you get one right," he said with that same little smile. "Two is good, three excellent and four outstanding."

The smile had become bigger. He didn't even mention five. He had thrown down the gauntlet, daring us. That Saturday, I worked on them all day and by late that night I had solved three. At two o'clock Sunday afternoon, I had the solution to the fourth problem, but no matter how hard I tried, I couldn't get the fifth. Late that night, Mother came downstairs.

"That's enough, now you go to bed," she ordered and I went.

I woke up at four in the morning with the solution. Somehow my brain had kept working while I was asleep. I sneaked downstairs but forgot the fifth step, the step Dad always avoided. The squeak woke Mother.

"What are you doing," she asked.

"I have the answer."

I was wide-awake, completed the solution to the problem, and went back to bed. On Monday morning, Mr. van Dop explained each problem on the black board and when he finished, he turned around and asked how many had solved one. A few hands went up.

"Who has solved two?" The majority of hands showed.

"Three?"

Six hands.

"Four?"

No hands.

He slowly looked the class over and lifted an eyebrow when he reached me. I nodded.

"Java Lane 4," he said.

When I rang his doorbell after school, he opened the door himself and led me to the inner sanctum, the living room. Tea. Mr. and Mrs. van Dop and I had tea and we talked, about school, the future, and they treated me as a friend.

"You know, Vetje told us all about you five years ago." His smile was real wide.

I loved that man.

My weakest subjects in high school were the foreign languages. We had two French teachers—little Miss Vinke and Miss Bijdendijk, she with the silk stockings. When she walked in the rows between the benches, we heard her legs rub against each other, swish, swish. As we grew older, we boys fantasized, the girls giggled. During orals of the final exam, these two ladies had a ball. For Dutch, German, and English, we had one of our own teachers and an outside observer, but the Germans didn't find that necessary for French. So the two ladies did it together.

"Translate this for me," Miss Vinke said.

I had some trouble with a sentence and Miss Bijdendijk whispered the translation to me. "Not so loud," Miss Vinke said. "I can hear you."

They both laughed and gave me a passing grade.

University was very much different from the HBS. No longer did we have teachers to guide us through classes, to help us individually and to keep discipline. In Utrecht, most students belonged to fraternities or sororities. They rowed, played tennis and field hockey, drank beer, and had parties. The most sought after fraternity was "de Soos," housed in a magnificent old building in the center of town. It was famous for its riotous parties. Being a student at a university was a time to have fun and some students took that literally. They never studied, flunked every exam, and stayed on year after year, making a profession out of being a student.

The students in Hilversum formed debating groups, a euphemism for having fun. Each group of eight was named after one of the muses and I was invited to join Terpsichore, the muse of dance, but not before another newcomer and I were hazed for a week. Terpsichore met every two weeks in the house of one of its members. We read poems early in the evening and when the beer began to have its influence, we switched to student songs, which included a famous German song:

Oh, you wonderful, wonderful little girl,
With your wonderful, wonderful blue eyes,
Yes, the eyes are yours,
But the looking into them is mine.

From the eyes, each subsequent couplet moved to lower regions of the anatomy. 'The lips so sweet to kiss,' 'the breasts so soft to feel' and so on. Five couplets in all. We invented ways to determine in whose house we would meet next. One evening, with our bladders full of beer, we assembled side by side on the balcony of the house of the president and let go in eight long streams into the fresh fallen snow down below. The next morning, we determined from the yellow stains whose urine had traveled the furthest and the lucky winner was to be our next host. It was my house.

Dad bought a keg of Heineken beer at his favorite bar and mother made snacks, which was not easy during wartime rationing. Eight young men crowded in my eight by nine foot room, which was not heated and had only an oil lamp for light. We sang our songs and drank the beer. Mother had decided that, when the time came to empty our bladders, instead of coming through the living room, it was easier for us to walk around outside to the back of the house where the toilet was located. It was no use arguing about it with her.

"You always tell people to walk outside to go to the bathroom?" a student remarked and I felt it. What bathroom? It was a toilet without water to wash your hands. When the keg was empty and they left, one student lingered.

"I like to thank your parents," he said.

The front door closed behind the others and I leaned against the wall, emotionally drained. They drove away on their bikes and one of them said, "Christ, how would you like to live like that?" He said it too loud, too soon. But it did not matter, because of Hans, the one who stayed behind.

I took him into the living room.

"Thank you, thank you very much for the hospitality, Mrs. Hoogstraten."

He was sincere. He didn't have to do it, but he knew that he would bring joy in doing it and Mother's face glowed. We had never thanked the parents, never met them. They were inconsequential to our get-together. Thanking them would have been met with a polite smile and, "You're quite welcome." Mother was tongue-tied. Dad had long gone to bed.

The next morning, Mother couldn't stop talking about what a nice young gentleman Hans was.

Besides the thoughts, there was the recurrent dream. It was a dream about two hands, hard hands with thick calluses and nails that never needed cutting or clipping. Bricks and mortar kept them short and on occasion a sharp pocketknife. From years of holding a two-foot square board loaded with mortar above the head with one hand and a heavy trowel in the other, the fingers could never again straighten and couldn't make a fist. Pieces of callus had fallen off the palms to expose pink rawness. Moisture had crept through the cracks in the callus and cement fungus had followed. Together it undermined the callus. Dirty bandages covered part of the pink. Black insulation strips, used by electricians to cover the ends of electric wire, hid the tips of some fingers. They were the hands of a bricklayer, a plasterer; the hands of my father.

145

11

A Peace Shattered

It happened. Our tranquility was shattered when on January 14, 1944, the same mysterious man who had brought Mrs. Sterk returned and asked to speak with her. Suddenly, all blood drained from Mrs. Sterk's face, her shoulders sagged, and a scared look came in her eyes. They went upstairs to the attic. At first we heard nothing, then a piercing scream, followed by uncontrolled crying. It seemed a long time before the man came downstairs and he explained that Mr. Sterk had been caught during a Nazi raid and now surely was on his way to a concentration camp. He left. We were dumbfounded. Bets stood with her hands to her mouth, Ann fixed her blind eyes on a spot on the ceiling, her chin jutting out, lips pressed in a thin line. I stood motionless, empty brained. This was terrible news. And then, as if one body, we went upstairs, sat on the edge of the bed with Mrs. Sterk, and shared our sorrow with her. Bets put an arm around her. We didn't say anything, just let her cry until there were no tears left and she could talk about her husband.

"He was a good man. He worked hard in his little business. He was good with the children. We have two children. People liked him."

On and on she went and it struck me that she was already talking as if her husband were dead. One short sentence after the other rolled out in a flat monotonous voice until finally she stopped, exhausted.

"I'll rest now," she said and laid down.

Bets stroked her hair, Ann bent over and gave her an awkward kiss on her ear, and I pulled the cover over her shoulders. We left in silence, sat around for a while, and went to bed in silence.

That night, I heard her cry again and I went upstairs and got in bed with her. She held me while she cried, shaking uncontrollably. After a while the crying became a soft whimper. I felt her body against me, the firm breasts. She fell asleep, a shake now and then, another whimper, and I stayed with her, warm, comfortable. At dawn, I crept out of her bed without waking her. She came downstairs late that morning and didn't eat breakfast. She cleared the table and disappeared into the kitchen, where she took a long time to wash the few dishes. In the afternoon, Bets and I listened to her as she talked about her family.

"This may be God's way of punishing me for my sins," she concluded.

I doubted that she had committed any sins other than little ones, sins one is allowed to forget.

"God does not punish," Bets said. "There is no punishing God, only a forgiving, loving God."

A faint smile came over Mrs. Sterk's face. "You know, we hardly ever went to the synagogue. I think I'll start going when this is over."

Dinner that night went by without a word, without much appetite, but the next morning, a different Mrs. Sterk came downstairs.

"Good morning," she said, her voice uplifting. "I have been thinking and have decided that my husband will want me to go on. I am going to survive this war and I'll be ready for my children when it's over."

She hadn't seen or heard from her children in nearly two years, but from somewhere she had found a new source of strength, and from that moment on we never saw her dispirited again. When she was upstairs in the attic later in the day, I talked to Bets.

"Can you let Mr. Loopstra know what happened? I'd like him to get the message to my parents."

"Why?"

Mine was a strange request, but I couldn't tell her about Mrs. Sterk's son. Mr. and Mrs Smale needed to be warned, just in case Mr. Sterk knew where his son was hidden. When the Germans tortured him beyond the limits of his endurance he might reveal the location.

"Please don't ask me to tell you why. Will you do it?"

She turned and looked at me, her head up, a bit to the side and her chin out, and it was clear that she was somewhat taken aback that I wouldn't take her in my confidence. Her eyelids moved quickly up and down a few times as if she was trying to clear her vision. "Yes, I will."

She put her coat on and left. With the fence as her guide, I saw her walk around the corner to Loopstra's house, a resolute little lady.

"He'll bring the message," she said upon her return and started reading, still a bit upset. I walked over to her and gave her a little hug. Five, ten seconds passed and then she patted my hand.

And then I went upstairs to Mrs. Sterk and told her the one thing that I felt she needed to know, that would help her. The words I really should not have said.

"Mrs. Sterk, I know that your son is safe and well."

She leaned over and grabbed my arm. "How do you know? Where is he?"

"I just know, but please do not ask more."

She looked at me for a while and then said, "I understand," she said. "But thank you for telling me."

12

Of Tea, Travel and Life

It became tradition for me to make tea on Sunday mornings and serve the three ladies a cup in bed, with a biscuit, if we had any. Only on Sunday morning, because that was the day when we still had real tea. First, I brought a cup to Mrs. Sterk, then three cups for Bets, Ann, and me. They were awake by that time and Bets usually sat upright on her side of the large bed, the side closest to the door. She brushed her long hair, stroke after stroke. Beautiful, shiny gray hair that she never washed. "Brush it and you'll never have to wash it. Dogs and horses don't wash and they are clean," she commented.

After giving Bets her cup, I moved around to Ann's side and the three of us drank our tea and talked. We never tired of talking. It was winter and very cold. One Sunday, Ann felt my hand when I handed her the cup.

"Wow, your hands are cold. Come sit next to me and put your legs under the blankets. Wrap this shawl around you."

"How stupid of us. Why didn't we think of that before?" Bets said.

So I sat in the bed next to Ann that Sunday and on the Sundays thereafter. Gradually, the sitting became lying down under the covers. Then, as the weeks passed, our sides touched, woman against man. And then, one day, Ann's hand moved over, feeling my chest, my nipples. The hand explored further, stomach, navel, pubic hair, pausing, hesitating and

149

then, very slowly, the penis. She continued talking. I lay motionless, speechless. Testicles, hardening. I tried not to react, but nature had its way. Pulsations, erecting, her hand soft, amazed at its discovery. She took my hand and put it on her breast, her small, never-used nipple getting firm. We lay until it passed. I kissed her briefly on the lips, got out of bed, walked over to Bets, kissed her on the forehead, and left the room.

"What was that all about?" I heard Bets say as I closed the door behind me.

The touching ran through my head for the rest of the week. I couldn't stop thinking about it. It could easily go further and then what? Where would it end? Ann was fifty-four years old and I wasn't even twenty. If this developed into a sexual relationship, would that mean that we had to marry? The thought alone scared me. It never occurred to me that two people could have sex without being married. Would Ann steer in that direction? And what about Bets? This was not my world, only one that I borrowed temporarily. This was Bets and Ann living in their blind world, together for more than fifty years. It couldn't be. And medical school—I had to become a doctor. I couldn't let anything interfere with that, couldn't let my family down. The microscope. All their pride had gone into that instrument. It was theirs and I was the custodian.

When a few days later Ann came to my room at night and put a hand on my shoulder, I pretended to be sleeping. She hesitated and left. Maybe she knew that I was not asleep or, just maybe, she hoped that I was asleep. Had she too been thinking? On the Sundays thereafter I brought a blanket from my bed to keep warm.

The sisters had a friend, Cor Zieren, an engineer in the coal mine Maurits. I never learned how they had become friends, or rather, how he and Ann had become friends. Bets always seemed rather cool to him. Mr. Zieren and his wife, a sickly woman, paid us a visit one-day and I thought that he acted rather possessive of Ann on that occasion. He didn't shower the same amount of attention on Bets, who seemed to prefer it that way. Something had been and still was going on and it was best for me to stay out of it. Two months later, Zieren called to say that his wife had died and Ann decided that she had to go to the funeral. I don't know why she felt compelled to go, but she had made up her mind. Bets seemed to understand. The question was how she was going to travel from Hilversum to where Zieren lived, in the very South of Holland, in Geleen, number 27 Prins de Ligne Street, the house next to the rectory of St. Augustinus church. Bets, the logical one, suggested that Ann and I travel together. We deliberated that idea for a while and it grew on us. It became something exciting, adventurous, especially for Bets, who wasn't even going. She made the plans. "Just tell them that you're blind when they stop you," she said. "We'll borrow two white canes and you must walk slowly. We might as well get some benefit from being blind." She laughed at her own joke, in short bursts, with head tilted, to the left.

The next morning, Ann and I took a taxi to the railroad station. The driver went out of his way to help us. Normally, the sisters shunned assistance, but for this trip, Bets had instructed us to act like two blind persons in need of help. At the station, the taxi driver took Ann's arm, told me to hold on to her other arm, and then guided us to the ticket office. Importantly, he stuck his head in the window and ordered the tickets.

"You be careful now," he said. "And when you come back, just call the Gooi Taxi and ask for me. I'll be right over." He completely forgot that we couldn't read his name on the license.

In Utrecht, the largest railroad center in the heart of Holland and a favorite place for the Germans and the Gestapo to

151

make arrests, we had to wait two hours for the train to Geleen. Arm in arm, we walked the platform, tapping the pavement with our canes as we went. A kind woman asked us where we were going.

"Can you please direct us to the restaurant?" Ann said.

"Oh sure, dear. Here, let me help you." She took Ann's arm. "Young man, you hold on to your mother's other arm."

Acting our part, we let her help us, stifling any laughter. Most people in the large waiting room were German soldiers on their way to a new posting or going home on leave. Three had Dutch girls with them—women of the moment who didn't mind being seen with the enemy. A high ranking officer and his wife sat to the side. At a table in a far corner, two Dutchmen leaned over their beer and talked in low voices. The Dutch tended to speak in rather loud voices, but during the war, when there were Germans or Dutch Nazis around, they didn't want to draw unnecessary attention. The lady took us to a table against a wall.

"There you are, out of the way here," she said. "Now keep a good eye on the clock, otherwise you'll miss your connection. Goodbye."

She left. Half way to the door she stopped, turned around, and came back to our table, all flustered.

"How dumb of me," she apologized. "I completely forgot that you couldn't see the clock, now can you. Tell me which train you're waiting for and I'll ask the waiter to let you know when it is time."

We told her and she went to the counter to talk with the waiter. She turned around and pointed at us. The waiter nodded and she left. At the door, she looked back at us and waved, but her hand stopped in midair. A smile came over her face, the hand came slowly down and she shook her head. Forgetful she was, the good soul. Little did she know that Ann had a special pocket watch that chimed the hour and quarter hours if she pressed a knob on its side. We always knew the approximate time and really didn't need to be warned, but it was part of our act not to know.

Three men entered the waiting room—two German soldiers, members of the military police, and a civilian in a long black leather coat, Gestapo no doubt. The Gestapo man stayed at the door while the soldiers began checking papers. Bets had insisted that we bring the small chess set along and we started a game, playing with unseeing eyes, feeling the pieces with our fingers.

"Ann, they're coming," I whispered.

"That's okay. We'll fool them," she said confidently.

They checked the soldiers first, then the two men in the corner, but they didn't disturb the high-ranking officer. The man in the black leather coat observed closely, looking for any abnormal reaction or nervousness on the part of anybody in the room, a give-away that something was wrong. Closer and closer they came until they reached our table.

"Ausweis," one of the soldiers growled at me.

I looked up at him, or rather, I fixed my eyes at the tip of his right ear. The other German looked at me, looked at Ann, took a closer look at the chessboard.

"Ach Heinz, die sind blind. Komm doch mal."

Heinz stared back at me and he seemed a little puzzled when our eyes didn't meet. Then he looked at Ann, at her hands moving over the pieces. Finally, it dawned on him.

"Verzeihung bitte," he said and clicked his heels.

"Poor devils," he said as they walked away. This from a man, who, without any feeling whatsoever, was responsible for sending Jews to their death in the gas chambers and unlucky Dutchmen without an Ausweis to German slave labor camps.

The rest of the trip went by without incident. In Geleen, Zieren welcomed us with open arms. He hovered over Ann, a bit too affectionately, I thought. Was I jealous? There was a daughter my age, Truus, who had already taken charge of the household during her mother's long illness, and a son Joep, two years older than I was. I was curious how he could move around freely without the Germans troubling him.

"How come they didn't pick you for a German labor camp?"

"That's easy. They badly need workers for the mine. As long as we produce coal which they can send to their country, they tend not to look too closely when they issue an Ausweis to a new worker."

A coal mine must be an ideal place to be truly underground, I thought. On the way back, in Utrecht, I saw Heinz and his partner again, checking papers on another platform. The Gestapo man stood off to the side.

"Ann, the same Germans are now on the other platform."

"Don't look," she said. "Keep walking."

Back home, Bets lived through every exciting moment with us.

"They are so stupid." She laughed.

The trip to Geleen made us bolder. One day, after dark, Ann and I stole a walk on the street outside. I picked a moment when we were not talking and intentionally let her stray towards a telephone pole. She stopped a few inches from the pole, felt in front of her, and touched it.

"Why did you do that?" she said, slightly annoyed.

"Ann, I wasn't going to let you walk into that pole. Honestly not. I only wanted to see whether you knew it was there, whether you could feel it."

"I felt it."

"But how?"

"I don't really know, but I felt that there was something in the way," she said with a dry smile. "Nobody ever did something like that with me. You know something, I'm amazed myself."

I also accompanied the sisters on two trips to Amsterdam, once to listen to a concert given by the Concert Gebouw Orchestra under the direction of Willem Mengelberg, and once to the music school on Anna Vondel Street. I'll never forget that concert, because it was the only time I ever saw a conductor stop the orchestra in the middle of a symphony—Beethoven's Eighth. A violinist struck a wrong chord, which was clearly heard by the knowledgeable audience. Mengelberg had the orchestra start all over again from the beginning. During the trip to the school, Ann wanted me to give a piano lesson to an advanced student, while she was busy with another student.

"Ann, I can't do that."

"Yes you can. Just let her play and tell her to make a few changes."

The student—a woman in her thirties—was an accomplished piano player. I stood behind her or walked around while she played, hands on my back as I had seen it done in the movies. When she was finished with a piece, I went over it with her. I acted blind, of course.

"I'd like you to build this section up more—more volume—and keep the tempo. You tend to rush it toward the end. Can you try that again?"

She did and liked it better. We did the same with a Chopin nocturne. When Ann came into the room at the end of the lesson, the student complimented me.

"He really has a good feeling for the music," she said. She turned to me. "Where did you study?"

Before I could answer, Ann said, "At the conservatory."

"How could you say a thing like that?" I said after the student had left.

"She never was at the conservatory." Ann laughed. "How would she know?"

"But why did you do it?"

"Do what?"

"Act as if I was a teacher."

"She is so insecure, she'll be taking lessons for the rest of her life and I'm getting bored with her. I really can't teach her anymore, only she doesn't realize it."

"Why don't you tell her?"

"That's no use. She'll only go to someone else."

We took the trolley to the railroad station for our train back to Hilversum. The Germans were checking papers again. We were walking briskly three abreast with me in the middle when I saw them at the gate to our platform. We were without white canes.

"Bets, Ann, there is trouble ahead. The Germans are checking papers."

It didn't faze the sisters one bit.

"We'll have to act being blind again," Bets said.

"Start shuffling," Ann said, and from a brisk step we changed into a slow, very cautious walk. Bets and Ann, chins up, moved their heads from left to right, mouths a little open, full of uncertainty, acting like helpless blind people to the hilt. I imitated them as best as I could and so we moved toward our gate. One of the Germans saw us coming. He held up one hand to halt the other passengers, nudged his partner to the side with the other hand, and let us through.

"Bitte."

"Danke schön."

No questions asked. We kept up our shuffling routine until we were in the train, and then had a good laugh. But that was the last time I went out with them.

On a warm summer day, Bets, Mrs. Sterk, and I were sitting in the dining room with the doors open to the garden, while upstairs Ann was giving a singing lesson to a rather heavy-set woman. She was our favorite student because she was one of two who lived on a farm and she always brought us something to eat.

"Dein ist mein Herz und soll es ewig bleiben," the woman bellowed. ("My heart is yours and will always be so.")

"No, no, no," a frustrated Ann exclaimed.

"It sounds as if she is shoving her heart on a platter across the table," I said.

"More like a cow calling the bull for mating." Bets chuckled.

"Poor bull," Mrs. Sterk added. We all laughed.

Bets, of all people, making that comment about the cow and the bull. Bets had never even seen a bull. From where did she get it? Later, I asked Mrs. Sterk about it and she made it clear to me.

"Even though they are blind, they are still two healthy women," she said. "And just like the girls in my high school talked about sex, they must have done the same with the other girls in the Institute. You know, just normal girl talk."

It may have been normal to her, but not to me. I thought that only boys talked about sex.

When a thunderstorm struck one evening I learned that the sisters didn't like it. After the first distant rumble, Ann, who was practicing for her next concert, immediately stopped playing. She slowly closed the piano lid and sat with her hands in her lap. Bets put her book down and sat like her sister. They waited quietly, quiet like the birds and leaves of the trees before a storm. With the first thunderclap, they both jerked vigorously and waited again. They again were startled with the second clap and then it dawned on me that they could not see the lightning and thus had no warning of the following thunder. They needed a break.

"Shall I tell you what happened when we were on vacation on the beach."

"Yes please," said Ann and she moved to her chair at the round table.

Bets' body and face relaxed. "I'll like that," she said.

———

157

Mrs. Sterk, eager for a distraction, joined us.

"We used to spend a few weeks the beach living in a tent and one weekend it was stormy weather. The word got out that the President of the Lifeboat Association had scheduled a practice of the lifeboat at five o'clock and the whole beach was caught up in the excitement. Already half an hour early we were waiting at the boathouse. Finally the heavy doors opened and we had our first glimpse of the boat. It was made of thick wooden boards joined in the center by a wide beam and she looked big and indestructible sitting high on its carrier. She was painted white on the outside and later we saw that she was red on the inside. It was a heavy, cumbersome boat giving a message of great strength and stability. The crewmembers—dressed in yellow oilskins and southwesters— look bigger than life. Their faces rugged, silent, they were oblivious to the crowd. They were proud men. And then we saw Kees, the tallest and strongest of them all. Kees, the vender, was our friend. Every day he came by with a yoke on his shoulders, a bucket of pickles at one end and herring at the other end. He was a tall, lanky fellow with a deep brown skin and big bare feet with which he could kick a soccer ball a mile.

"There's Kees. Hey Kees!" we yelled.

But that day Kees ignored us. He was busy jawing with the other rowers, waiting for the horses to arrive. Off to the side stood the President of the Association and the other gentlemen of the board, all dressed in their Sunday best. The President was talking to a small man, the helmsman. Then the horses came—big, strong horses used to pulling heavy loads in the field. Their owners handled them personally, because for this important occasion no hired hand would do. These were specially selected horses—volunteers you might say, just like the rowers—and the owners exuded the same nonchalant pride as the crew did. There was a serious job to be done. They harnessed the horses to the carrier and on a sign from the helmsman they began to pull. The rowers walked alongside the boat, six on each side. Their waist-high boots made them take longer steps than normal, big plodding steps that went well with the boat.

It was easy going down the cobblestones leading from the boathouse to the beach, but when they reached the end of the path, the wide, steel-rimmed wheels of the carrier sank deep in the fine dune sand and they came to an abrupt halt. Horses leaned into their leather harnesses, hoofs clawed and slipped, handlers cursed and whipped. Horses snorted, whinnied and shuddered, and the carrier didn't move.

The leading horses were two magnificent black stallions. Their muscles rippled under wet, velvet coats. They were not as big and heavy as the other horses, but seemed less nervous. Their owner, a small man, moved in between his animals and spoke to them in a quiet voice.

"Steady Brutus, steady Cleo. Steady boys."

He turned around and took a firm grip on their bridles. Brutus and Cleo seemed to gather themselves for what was coming.

"Now boys, now."

With eyes bulging and wild, their nostrils wide open red against black and with froth breaking out they dug in. The owners of the other horses still cursed and whipped, but it was no longer necessary. The animals sensed what was going on up ahead. No longer nervous, quiet now, they began to pull as a team and slowly the big wheels began turning again, creaking. They reached the hard sand and from then on moved along the beach at a steady pace, a festive pace. Children ran alongside, laughing, chasing each other, and adults followed, free to talk.

At pole eighteen they stopped, turned left and faced the turbulent water. The rowers climbed aboard and the skipper took his place at the helm. The horses were rearranged alongside the boat, their handlers straddled their wide backs and on command of the helmsman they moved forward. They pulled the carrier into the first surf until the water reached their bellies and then came up again on the first bank. Encouraged by the handlers, they moved into the second surf. When the water rolled over their shoulders and their necks were stretched out high, they halted. The handlers, still sitting on their backs, unhooked them and drove them back to the beach.

The helmsman, an old fisherman, studied the incoming waves carefully, waiting for the right one to form. Then, on his command, the rowers strained their backs and pulled the oars as one when the wave reached the carrier. Off they went, climbing the waves and falling down the water slopes, getting smaller as they went until the boat was nothing more than a white dot. And then there was nothing.

The carrier was left where it was. On the beach the two black stallions stood apart from the other horses as if they were special, their muscles still twitching from the strain. It wasn't until two hours later that the boat returned and the horses were driven back in the stormy sea. One more critical moment and then, as if by magic, the boat once again rested on the carrier. On the way back, the rowers walked silently beside their boat, their steps shorter now, their backs bent and faces lined with fatigue. We walked with Kees and said not a word. Our hero."

I finished the story and the thunderstorm had passed over.

"Thank you," said Ann. "We needed that."

"Yes we did and I liked the horses." Bets always went for the animals.

Mrs. Sterk came over and planted a firm kiss on my cheek.

One evening, after dinner, Ann was practicing for the piano concert she gave once a year for her students, friends, and anyone willing to pay the price of a ticket. She played

'The Appassionata' by Beethoven, while Bets read and I converted something into Braille.

"I don't like it," Ann interrupted her playing, "Something isn't right. Barth, what do you think?"

I sat next to her and she played the section again.

"Ann, this is a strong piece and I don't think that you let that strength come out," I said.

She tried it again. "I like it better that way," she said.

That was the first and only time I saw Bets angry.

"You never accept critique or suggestions from me, and now he comes along and you listen to him!" She stormed out of the room and actually slammed the door.

"She'll cool down," Ann remarked dryly. "Let's continue."

But I couldn't. "No, Ann, Bets is right. You don't listen to her advice and she is your sister. Besides, she knows far more about music than I do." Ann played on for a while, hitting the keys harder than usual, it seemed. After a while, she stopped abruptly, got up, and left the room. In bed that night, my thoughts went back to that episode. It was understandable that Bets had been annoyed with her sister at that moment, but hadn't she reacted too vehemently? Was there more to it than Ann accepting my advice? Had my entering into their lives changed the dynamics of the sisters' relationship? Was it my fault? There was nothing between Ann and me, but I did enjoy her physical presence. She radiated toward me and she might be doing that to others as well, but I wasn't there to notice, so I didn't know. Her giving impacted me and I liked it. Did I have the same effect on her, and did Bets notice? The questions kept on popping up in my mind and I couldn't find answers. It was a long time before I fell asleep, but not before I decided to give more of myself to Bets from now on.

The next morning, when Ann drove by the house on her way to the Institute, I hit a key on the piano as I did every

161

day. This time she didn't turn her head, nor did I see her laugh, which was always a sure sign that she had recognized the note. She was silent when she returned home in late afternoon and remained so throughout dinner. However, I felt that it wasn't a defiant silence. There was softness to it. A tear welled in her right eye and slowly began to find its way down her cheek. Not a word was said. Bets lifted her head sideways in three small jerking motions and turned to where her sister was sitting. She stood up, groped her way around the table, strangely insecure of her movements, felt for Ann's shoulder, and gave her three little pats on the head. Ann stood up as well, her tears now running freely, and hugged Bets and left the room, closing the door softly.

"She'll be all right now," Bets said, her voice a little hoarse.

From then on rehearsing became a three-way street, with suggestions from Bets and me, in that order.

13

The Raid and the Coal Mine

The days and weeks went by—summer, fall, winter, and spring. Our only communication with the outside world came through the Nazi-controlled radio and whatever news Ann brought back from her trips to the Institute. The radio announced that the victorious German army had begun another strategic shortening of the Russian front, but by adjusting the pins on our map to the towns that had fallen under Russian control, we knew that the Germans were losing and falling back. Bets, as usual, had a sarcastic remark about the announcement of yet another "elastic withdrawal." She called it "backward strategy." The number of big Allied planes flying overhead on their way to Germany increased to the thousands, and so we knew that the war was going better for us. Outside, the streets had become eerily quiet. Now and then I recognized a girl from high school as she rode by the house on her bike, but no cars passed our street. No boys my age ever drove by.

Once, in mid April, I saw the Nazi high school custodian, van Drie, on his bike. He looked at our house, but I was sure that he couldn't see me, because I was standing deep within the room. A few weeks later, I saw him again from my bedroom window and I had a strange feeling in the pit of stomach. Was this more than coincidental? After Mrs. Sterk went upstairs that night, I told the sisters about it.

"Did he see you?" Ann asked.

"I don't think so. The first time, I was deep within the room and the lights were not on. The second time I was upstairs and he didn't look up."

"It's probably a coincidence."

"Maybe, but we better be more careful from now on. No more playing a note on the piano Ann, when you leave in the morning."

Bets was concerned about Mrs. Sterk.

"We can't tell her. She'll be scared to death. Do you think that we ought to tell the man who brought her here?"

"How? We don't know his name or where he lives. There's no way that we can contact him." It was a helpless feeling.

After a long silence, Ann still thought that this was the safest place for Mrs. Sterk.

"They're not going to look here. Everybody knows that we're blind."

"Nevertheless, I think we need to tell her what happened," I said. "She ought to know and she too should be careful."

I went upstairs to the attic and told her about van Drie and my discussion with the sisters. She took it very calmly.

"I agree with Ann. This is the safest place for me and I just can't run again. This house has been too good to me and I really can't face yet another change. It's too nerve wracking. I can't take it again. I'll stay and take what comes. Maybe it was all a coincidence."

Sunday, May seventh, 1944, at noon, we had finished playing as a trio, only this time there was no audience. I was standing in the front room, Bets was in the bathroom, Ann was upstairs in her bedroom, and Mrs. Sterk was in the attic. Suddenly, a German army truck came racing around the corner of Nassau Avenue and screeched to a halt in front of our house. Soldiers, rifles at the ready, jumped out and ran in all directions towards our house. Clearly, this was not the ordinary mass raid for which we had prepared ourselves these past months. This was a targeted daytime raid and that meant only one thing—we had been betrayed. They were either after Mrs. Sterk or after me and this was not the time to find out which. There was no way that Mrs. Sterk could get into the hole and it would make no sense for me to pretend that I was blind. Those thoughts raced through my mind as I yelled from the top of my voice, "Raid! Raid!"

I ran out of the kitchen door, clawed up the back fence, rolled over, and ran through one backyard after another. Near the last house on Nassau Avenue, I stopped to catch my breath and to calm down. Where to go? My original idea of going to Uncle Jaap was suddenly out of the question. There was no way I could get to Kortenhoef, which had no train or bus connection from Hilversum. I had to get out of town fast and walking or cycling weren't options. I found my way to the small adjunct railroad station, where Groeneveld, the keeper of the bicycle shed, recognized me as a student.

"What are you doing here?"

"There is a raid on the house where I was hiding. I have to get away."

He hid me in the shed, while I waited for the train to Utrecht.

"Let me first talk to the conductor before you come out," he said. "Wait for my signal."

When the train arrived, Groeneveld walked to the platform and spoke with the conductor. After a while, he looked back and nodded. I walked to the last car and hopped in. It was practically empty. The conductor came by some time later.

"Where are you going?" He didn't ask for my ticket, knowing that I didn't have one.

"I want to go to my aunt in Utrecht."

"That's not a good idea. The Germans are checking pa-

165

pers at every exit of the station and there's no way you can leave the station without an Ausweis."

There had been no time to get my identity card or the letter from the Director of the Institute. I was no longer blind.

"Thanks. I'll have to think of something else."

I thought about it for a while, and then the discussion I had with Joep Zieren came to mind. I had to get to Geleen. And I remembered that cousin Henk now was an engineer with the railroad. When we arrived in Utrecht, I walked to the nearest locomotive and asked the engineer whether he knew Henk van der Velde. He did.

"I'm his cousin and I'm on the run. Can you help me?"

Railroad workers were known throughout Holland as being fiercely anti-German and this man was no exception. He took a quick look at the now empty platform.

"Hop in." He immediately closed the cabin door behind me. "Where do you want to go?"

"To Geleen."

He whistled softly. "Geleen. That won't be easy. That's a long way from here."

He scratched his head and consulted with his mate. "What do you think, Gerrit?"

Gerrit, who didn't look much older than me, also went through the motion of scratching his head and winked at me.

"I think we can arrange it. You want me to find out?"

"No, you stay with him and I'll see what I can do."

He climbed down from the cabin and disappeared.

"What happened?" Gerrit said.

"Oh, they raided the house in which I was hiding and I managed to escape."

"How long have you been underground?"

"Little over a year."

"Must be rotten, cooped up like that."

"You get used to it."

It seemed a long time before he came back with another engineer, who carried a bundle of railroad overalls and a cap under his arm. "Put these on," he said. They had arranged for me to ride in the locomotive of the train to Eindhoven, where I transferred to the train for Roermond. Dressed in overalls, with a cap on my head and with coal dust smudges on my hands and face, I looked like an assistant engineer. In Roermond, I was handed over to a train for Sittard, and then to a fourth one for Geleen. Every time the engineers walked me to the next locomotive. After a short explanation, it was "Hop on" without further questions being asked.

When we arrived in Geleen, the last engineer took me to the crew shack.

"Keep the overalls on and the cap. You better stay here until it's dark before walking the streets." He explained how I could find Prins de Ligne Street and left. The events had come so fast that I hadn't had time to think until now. They had caught Mrs. Sterk for sure, but what about Bets and Ann? Would their blindness protect them and would Bets' explanation about the presence of a Jewish woman in her house hold up? "How could we know that she was a Jew? Nobody told us." The Germans had surely found some of my clothes and had asked whose they were. The sisters could tell them that they belonged to a blind student who lived with them and wasn't home right then. But would they find my identity card and letter from the Institute? I was pretty sure that Bets would come up with an answer if they asked about them. "He forgot them again," she would say. "He always forgets something."

The sisters might be blind, but they were as strong, if not stronger, than other women were and very brave. The longer I thought about them and about the raid, the more confident I became that they would make out all right. They were not only excellent musicians, but also good actors. I wasn't worried about what would be in store for me. Other than know-

167

ing that I would be a doctor one day, I hadn't troubled to think ahead while I was with Bets and Ann, never figured out all possibilities. It wasn't worth it. Nothing was for sure in those days, anyway.

The streets were completely deserted when I found my way to Prins de Ligne Street, which wasn't surprising, because it was after the curfew hour when I left the railroad shack. Truus opened the door when I rang the bell. No men ever opened the door at night—only women. Germans and Dutch Nazis weren't after the women. She peered at my face, trying to remember who I was from the short visit during her mother's funeral, when she had so many other things on her mind.

"It's Barth. I was here with Ann Frank last year."

"Come in," she said with a faint smile of recognition.

In the warm living room, a surprised Mr. Zieren rose from his easy chair near the fireplace. There obviously was no shortage of coal in that mining town. Joep, the twenty-two year old son, eyed me with slight suspicion.

"Barth, what are you doing here?" Mr. Zieren said.

I explained what had happened in Hilversum—the daylight raid, my escape, and why I couldn't go to my aunt in Utrecht. He immediately went to the phone to call the sisters. We overheard the one-sided conversation.

"Bets! Thank goodness you are safe. What happened? Uh—uh."

A long pause. I was relieved to hear the good news that they were safe.

"And Mrs. Sterk?"

Another pause.

"I'm sorry to hear that. Well, uh, we have a visitor. I don't think you and Annie know him. A nice young man with the darnest red hair you have ever seen. Uh—uh. Say hello to Annie. Bye."

"They are okay, but they took Mrs. Sterk," he said after he hung up.

168

"I thought so," I said. "There was no way she could have escaped. I was barely able to get over the fence."

"They asked something about some clothes in your room, but evidently they were satisfied with the explanation."

"What about my false identity papers? They must have found those."

"Bets didn't mention them. Now, how about you? Do you have any plans?"

"No, but on the way here, I started thinking. Is it possible to go really underground, in the coal mine I mean?"

He laughed.

"There is no need for that here. Joep is your age and he didn't have to go underground. He works in the mine like so many other younger men. The Germans are all too happy with any man willing to work there. As long as we produce the coal, they leave us alone. I'll get you a job tomorrow. And you can stay here with us, but we have to get you an Ausweis and food stamps."

There never was any hesitation, not a moment of doubt. I was welcome for as long as necessary. Joep, who hadn't said a word thus far, came alive after he heard my story.

"I'll take care of the Ausweis. The food stamps are easy. They come with the job."

"Truus will show you your room upstairs. I assume that you have no other clothes than the ones you are wearing. Joep, will you give him some of yours?"

The next morning, Joep called from the mine to say that I should report to the personnel office and ask for Mr. Pietersen. It was a short walk to the mine. A German soldier stopped me at the main gate, but when I told him that I was reporting for work, he asked no questions and pointed me to the personnel office. Mr. Pietersen gave me a quick look and then put his head down.

"Zieren told me you were coming." Then, in a low voice,

"Do as if we're talking otherwise the fellow over there will become suspicious."

The only other person in the office was a dour looking man at a corner desk.

"Wait here. I'll get the necessary papers." Pietersen left.

I took a chair along the wall and avoided looking at the man at the other desk. But I kept in him in view from the corner of my eyes. After a while he stood up and looked at me. I gave him a smile. He started to walk over to me and I recognized the Nazi button in the lapel of his jacket. Just then Mr. Pietersen returned. He quickly took in the situation and walked to his desk.

"Everything is in order. You are a diesel fitter. Tomorrow morning, you report for work in the main repair hall. Here are your food coupons. Your lunch is free at the cafeteria. This here is your temporary Ausweis. It'll take a while before you get a permanent one. "

The other man had gone back to his desk.

"That was close," Pietersen whispered. "Do you have an identity card?"

"No, sir. It was stolen from me in the train." I too kept my voice down. It wasn't a good lie, but that was the best I could come up with so quickly.

He asked a few details about me and took a photo.

"Come back in three days. Good luck."

He never looked up at me again and I left without saying another word. It was only later that I learned that he and Joep worked in the underground together. When I came back three days later, he handed me my new identity card. The foreman in the repair hall found me a spot on a long work-bench, between two old timers. They looked at my milk white hands and decided to have some fun.

"Barth, that's your name, right? Well, Barth, why don't you go to Tom over there and ask for a feather hammer."

I smiled, remembering the baptism I underwent on my first day on the job with Dad, when the workers also sent me on a wild goose chase for some imaginary hammer. "Is that the same kind of hammer as one with a half-ball head?" They laughed, knowing that I had found them out. They tried once more that afternoon, but I was waiting for it. They had put a thin layer of grease on the head of my hammer. Fellow can really hurt his left thumb, when the hammer slips. "I wonder how that grease got on my hammer?" I said in a loud voice and looked around, grinning. They grinned back and soon I became one of theirs. The work was dull—cleaning the grooves for the piston rings of the diesel locomotives that were used for transportation deep down in the mine, nearly ten thousand feet down at the deepest point. That's where Joep worked, most of the time lying on his back in long, two feet high side channels. He was looking for new coal veins, chipping away at the hard rock. Now and then he hit a water vein instead and received an unwelcome bath with ice cold water. It was hard work, crawling and working in those narrow tunnels, the work for young men.

Joep never said much. He worked the night shift, slept until late in the afternoon, and only shared dinner with us. I had the feeling that he and his dad didn't get along too well. One lived and worked above ground, the other deep underground. Mr. Zieren was a precise man. He spoke in short, clipped sentences, wore a suit, clean white starched shirt and tie, and read the newspaper. He led an orderly life, a clean life. His son hardly ever talked at home. He wore his trousers with a rope for belt, a colored shirt open at the neck and his fingernails were black from coal dust. He was a strong man, one who knew what he wanted and got it.

Nobody worked hard at the mine. During the four years of German occupation, the work force at the mine had tripled and yet it managed to bring less than half the amount of coal to the surface than it did before the war. Minor forms of annoying sabotage were a daily occurrence and it was amazing how such minor sabotage could lead to a complete work stoppage in the various departments of the mine. Deep down in the earth, there was no need for sabotage. Most of the time the miners simply didn't work. They sat around talking or playing cards. Engineer Fransen, the Dutch Nazi supervisor, once said something about it, but that same day he was met by three black-faced miners in a dark corridor at six thousand feet. They beat him up pretty good and Fransen kept his mouth shut from then on. No German dared go down below. That was a tough territory.

The day after the Normandy invasion, we had a serious 'accident' in the main repair hall. The hall was huge, the size of several football fields, and in the center hang an enormous crane that ran the entire length of the hall. Its operation was simple, with five chains hanging down from the control. Each chain had a colored wooden handle at the end. Pull on the green handle and the crane moved forward; pull the red one and it came back. The blue handle brought the hook down and the yellow one pulled it up. The black handle stopped everything. We also had a Nazi supervisor in our hall, a rather nice man, who wasn't out to make trouble for us. He had been appointed shortly after Mr. Fransen had that rather unfortunate little accident down below and he understood what was good for him. He stayed all day in his little office and said nothing.

The usual crane operator reported sick on the eventful day. His substitute had just hooked on a locomotive at one end of the hall. When he rode the crane down to where we were working and pulled the black handle, the crane continued on its way down the hall. The alarm went off, the supervisor ran to the assistance of the crane operator and pulled the black handle with him, but the chain didn't budge. We all looked on with great anticipation, knowing what would happen next. When the crane reached the end of the hall at full speed, it went right through the wall and crashed on the road outside. Forewarned, nobody happened to be in its way. It took weeks before the damage was repaired and it slowed the work down considerably. The cause of the 'accident' turned out to be a knot in the chain. "It must have twisted somehow," the supervisor said. We all agreed with that assessment.

In August, I received a message from Mr. Pietersen that my Ausweis was ready. I traveled to the regional labor office in Heerlen, where a clerk handed me the valuable piece of paper. It still required a signature for which he directed me to a glass door. Behind a large desk, a hunchbacked German in uniform and a much too large cap did the formalities. He wanted to see my old Ausweis, which I claimed to have had in Hilversum, but I was prepared for the trick question. An Ausweis was printed in large, bold letters, so that the Germans could easily read it. Below it, in faint and very small print, was the Dutch translation, one of which said that the owner had to turn the Ausweis in when he changed jobs. I told the hunchback that I had turned it in when I left Hilversum, figuring that with the American army racing out of Normandy, he had more important things on his mind than checking my credentials. He signed. Here, in the most Southern part of Holland, nobody knew me and I was again using my real name. As a result, I now was the not-so-proud owner of an Ausweis, a yellowish piece of paper with a brown border. My Ausweis number was 2 339928 and it stated that "Hoogstraten, Bartholomeus, born on 13 May, 1924 in Loosdrecht (U), living in Geleen (L), single, identity card H 78/ 022367, has according to regulation been registered for labor employment and with permission from the Regional Labor Office by the firm Stm. Maurits, Geleen, worknr. 7997 as diesel fitter employed."

173

The Auswies

The translation is somewhat awkward. There are no Dutch words for some of the pompous German words such as 'Arbeitseinsatz.'

Life with the Zierens was uneventful. After Mr. Zieren came home from work at the mine and finished the evening meal, he withdrew into his easy chair next to the fireplace to read or doze off. Truus, 19 years old, was an angel. She kept the house going, prepared the meals, played commendable piano, and sang with a lovely voice. And I read. For more than a year, I had been starved of reading and I now went through every book in the house. In the meanwhile, the allied armies continued their march through France and we became more and more excited at the prospect of being liberated in the now foreseeable future. But not before disaster nearly struck Geleen on a large scale.

174

The pilots of two British fighter planes mistook Geleen for a German town and, in three passes, perforated the two metal skins of a huge gas storage tank with their bullets. The tank, which was located on the grounds of the mine, easily measured eighty feet in diameter and was sixty feet high. One or more bullets had ignited the gas, which was now burning off, and the inner shell of the container with its heavy roof came slowly down. If it kept going down, there would be little danger, but the inner shell might get hung up on the ragged edges of the bullet holes any time and when that happened, a vacuum would be created, which could result in a massive explosion.

The mine alerted the mayor of Geleen, who ordered an immediate evacuation. The population had two ways to go—either out of town or hide in the enormous slack pile across the street from the mine. The pile was a natural bomb shelter. People had dug channels deep into its heart and some families even lived in it permanently. Many a child was conceived in that pile. When gas is removed from the coal it turns into slack, which was transported in a long chain of tipcarts to the top of the slack pile. There they dropped their load and turned around for another load. Every day the mountain grew higher. There was always a danger that pieces of slack might drop while the tipcarts moved high across the street and, in order to prevent accidents, a steel wire netting had been stretched just below the carts to catch the falling pieces. It was that wire mesh that became important.

Mr. Zieren, who was in charge of safety at the mine, asked for two volunteers to climb on the netting, walk as close as possible to the gas container and report on the progress of the roof of the container on its way down, which could only be seen from above. Joep immediately volunteered and I joined him. Armed with binoculars, we found our way onto the wire mesh, crossed high above the street, and came to a point close enough to observe the slow slide of the inner shell. It was windy up there and with sudden gusts we had to hold on for dear life. We saw several bullet holes and the roof, on its way down, had flattened out the ragged edges. As long as it kept doing that, there was no danger. Every fifteen minutes, Joep or I walked back to yell down a progress report. Fortunately, the slide down of the inner shell never stopped and after five hours most of the gas had burned off and the people could go back to their homes.

The episode with the gas container was just the beginning of several exciting weeks to come. At least it was exciting for a young man like me. The next day, Joep called me into his bedroom.

"Barth, I like what you did yesterday."

"Come on, that was no big deal. Anybody could have done that. You did."

"The point is, not anybody volunteered. Anyway, I know I can trust you. I am a member of a resistance group and I'd like you to join us. With the war coming to an end, the Germans and the Dutch Nazis are getting very nasty and we can use more good men."

He didn't give any more details and I knew better not to ask. He also didn't have to ask me twice. For some time, deep down, I had harbored a guilt feeling that I hadn't been more active in fighting the Germans. While I was underground in relative safety with Bets and Ann, the Nazi controlled Dutch radio increasingly reported on the terrorist activity by Dutch resistance groups. They called it terrorist action—we called it resistance fighting. My inactivity had begun to bother me.

"I would like nothing better," I said.

"Good. From now on you must have a code name, because for safety sake we only know each other by code names. I am known only as Jack."

"I'll take Ernst." I stuck to my old name.

"All right, I'll introduce you as Ernst. No last names, no addresses."

He told me to be ready at all times. Many stories about the activities of the resistance made the rounds amongst ordinary citizens, but few were actually confirmed during the war. Strict secrecy was the operative word. People liked to talk about them, though. It made them feel better, gave them pride, even when they didn't really know what exactly was going on. Of all the stories going around, the underground did confirm one rumor, perhaps to reinforce the pride. It was about a girl who had repeatedly acted as a decoy while the resistance fighters did their act. She was caught and severely tortured by the Gestapo. After several weeks of torture, during which she refused to reveal the names of the other people in her resistance cell, she was put on a train to Germany under heavy guard and, during that trip, the resistance managed to free her. A few days later, the BBC sent a coded message that she had arrived safely in England. A story like that made everybody feel good and it strengthened the will power of the people.

I didn't have to wait long for a call from Joep. The American army was rapidly advancing through Belgium and the Germans were in full retreat. The remnants of a panzer division were one of the last units to come through Geleen. The tanks stopped at the mine to load up on the diesel oil used for the locomotives. The oil was stored in a large underground tank behind the repair hall. Joep had quickly analyzed the situation and volunteered himself and me to work the hand pump with which the oil could be brought to the surface.

"Helping the Germans? What does he have in mind?" I wondered.

A middle-aged soldier rolled an empty barrel to the pump and we began pumping. Joep quickly threw handfuls of sand in the barrel, when the soldier left to get another one. By the time that he returned with the empty barrel, we had the first one filled. He rolled it to the tanks, where the tank crew loaded it on the back of their tanks. I don't know how many barrels we filled that day, but one thing was sure, those tanks didn't go very far with sand in their engines. It wasn't very glamorous sabotage, but certainly was effective.

The Germans were determined that the advancing allied armies would make no use of the modern mine Maurits. Either that or they were in a resentful, destructive mood. Why else would they destroy the mine? They placed bombs at the most strategic point of the mine—the powerhouse with the dynamos. From many veins deep down, water flowed continuously into a mine and if it was not pumped out, the mine would fill up with water, a process called 'drowning the mine.' The Germans knew this and they also knew that the electricity to work the pumps and the rest of the mine was generated by the eight large dynamos in the power plant. They wired a bomb to each dynamo, put sandbags around them, and placed soldiers on guard at the doors of the powerhouse day and night.

The resistance decided to save the mine from destruction, because the rest of the country needed our coal as soon as it was liberated. Joep and two members of his group managed to slip into the building while a charming girl distracted the guard at the back door. Once inside, they began to deactivate the bombs by clipping a piece from the wires leading to the detonator and inserting a piece of fake wire in its stead. I served as a lookout in case an officer or other German unexpectedly approached and noticed the unguarded door. One member of the group, who had slipped inside the building, kept his eyes fixed on me from a window. An officer did approach. I quickly signaled the man inside and walked to the officer.

"Guten Morgen," I smiled. "Haben Sie ein Cigarette bitte?" I never smoked.

The officer, not used to such friendliness from a Dutchman, took a pack from his breast pocket and offered me one. He even lit my cigarette and we struck up a conversation. In the meanwhile, the three men inside had time to slip out and the girl walked the guard back to his post. The group had managed to deactivate the bombs of the two largest dynamos and of a third smaller one. They also alerted the allies about the bombs. When the last German out pulled the switch, only five dynamos were damaged and within a week after the liberation of Geleen, new dynamos arrived via France and Belgium from Switzerland. The mine stayed dry.

14

We are Free!!

Any day now it could happen. Liberation, freedom at last. For the past two days, we had heard the sound of gunfire come closer, and our excitement was growing. From a secret hiding place in the attic, Cor Zieren pulled a bottle of wine he had saved for four years and four months. News reached us that Maastricht was free and we were only a few miles to the North. On September 18, 1944, it was the early morning of a beautiful day. I walked out of the front door and looked at an empty street. Front doors opened everywhere and people came out of their houses.

"What is happening?" the woman next door said. "It's so quiet."

Then it struck me, too. There was no noise. The guns had fallen silent. Suddenly a crazed young German officer on a stolen bicycle stopped at the corner of our street and Main Street.

"Hinein, gehen Sie hinein," he yelled.

The people were confused.

"What is he saying?" our neighbor asked.

"He wants us to go back inside," I translated, but the people remained standing in their front yards, curious as to what was going on. That changed fast when the officer pulled a gun and started to shoot wildly down the street. We all hustled back inside. The German moved on, going north, keeping a safe distance between himself and the Americans.

The owner of the house on the corner cautiously walked into his front yard and looked.

"He is gone," he yelled and once again all doors opened. Mr. Zieren had already left for work and Joep was sound asleep. Truus joined me outside. The mood of the people milling in the street was feverish. Someone put the Dutch flag in a window.

"The flag, we can fly our flag," a woman yelled, and suddenly flags appeared from everywhere—the red-white-and blue, with an orange pennant. Solemnly, a man started to sing our national anthem, "Wilhelmus van Nassau" and we all joined in. Tears were streaming down faces, grown men cried without shame, and I had a big lump in my throat, close to tears myself. It was here. We were free! We were free! I hugged Truus, hugged women I had never seen before, happy women, crying women, and I was kissed on cheeks and lips and gave kisses.

"Listen! Listen!" someone yelled. Everybody listened. The sound of engines grew rapidly louder and before we knew it, two Harley Davidson motorcycles came roaring around the corner into our street. They didn't get very far. People ran to them from all sides and surrounded two smiling American soldiers. People came from everywhere—children, young and old women and men, and in no time, the Americans were lost in the middle of a hysterically happy mob. Bottles of wine and champagne appeared as if there never had been a shortage. People drank, children drank, and two dusty American scouts with goggles high on their helmets and still sitting on their bikes, drank. The bravest girls kissed them and they were happy.

"Thanks for coming," I said to one of them. It sounded so formal, like I welcomed a friend at a cocktail party, but it was all I could think of at the moment. Most Dutchmen had learned to speak English in high school, but we had been out of practice for five years. He winked at me. And then it was time for them to move on. We warned them.

"Be careful. About a mile North of town, at the cross-roads, the Germans have an 88-mm anti-aircraft gun and a machine gun nest. The gun barrel is aimed down the road, not into the sky."

They laughed, turned their big bikes around, and roared away, cowboys on wheels. Moments later, we heard the familiar barking of a German machine gun. Two sons of America would no longer ride their bikes, would no longer feel arms of young happy girls around their necks, nor enjoy the kisses of women they had just liberated. The crowd fell silent, knowing.

"Oh my God, why didn't they listen? Why?"

Our happiness dissipated just as fast as it had begun. The same salty tears of happiness now flowed in sorrow.

"I just kissed him," a girl cried on the shoulder of her friend standing next to me.

We were free, but we no longer felt like celebrating. Death, the awfulness of war had struck home for a last time. The people didn't return to their homes. Joep, who had awakened from all the noise, joined us. We all stood on the street and talked. We talked long enough for the sorrow to lessen and gradually we became happy again. Only it was a different kind of happiness, no longer hysterical . . . it was a thankful happiness.

Thirty minutes later we heard new, heavier engine sounds and the clanking of steel tracks. The tanks were coming. We all faced the end of the street, waiting for the first one to round the corner. Suddenly, a tank appeared between two houses, and then another, and another. They rolled through carefully kept Dutch gardens and mowed down the little fences. They rolled across the street, over the fences on the other side, through the gardens and disappeared between the houses. A scout car stayed behind and the soldiers inside talked to us.

"Why did you guys come through the gardens?" Joep asked one of them.

"We heard that the Krauts have an 88-mm at a corner. We didn't know which one and we never take chances with an 88. So we stayed away from street corners."

"But they may have killed the scouts," I said.

"Let's hope not. At least they managed to get the message off," he said.

That afternoon Joep, a friend and I went to the crossroad. The machine gun nest was blasted to pieces and the long barrel of the 88 hung down at a grotesque angle. There were two freshly dug, shallow graves, each with an upside down rifle and a helmet on top.

When we came back in town, we found it in uproar. A large crowd was screaming, laughing, and spitting at eight young women. The emotion of the liberation had unleashed all their hatred and pent-up anger at these eight well known Nazi whores. Two men and women were shaving their heads none too gently and when they were finished the crowd paraded the women through town, but not before putting signs around their necks that read 'I am a Nazi whore.' They walked with their hands behind their neck until they reached the town hall. There one of the women defiantly made the Hitler salute and was immediately knocked down by a man. The crowd surged forward but the police held the people off. They quickly grabbed the now pathetic women and put them in holding cells until a decision was made what to do with them next.

All but one of the mine supervisors appointed by the Germans had long left Geleen, but one stayed behind in his house.

"Fransen is still here," someone yelled. A bunch of coal miners went out to get him.

___

183

I followed, curious about what they would do to the man. Without paying attention to his hysterically crying wife, they pulled him out of his house and paraded him through town. He, too, was forced to keep his hands behind his head and when he didn't move fast enough to their taste, they kicked him so that he started running with fear in his eyes. People tried to punch or kick him as he ran the gauntlet. Women and children pelted him with mud and ashes. Short of the town hall, he fell down, totally exhausted, the fear replaced by a sullen acceptance of his fate. A burly mine worker pulled him up and the last hundred yards he was forced to crawl to the steps of the town hall. There, the chief of police had pity with him. He had only been a minor figure, thrown in a position of power by his party bosses, power he hadn't dare use deep down in the mine after he had received that beating.

Late in the evening, the doorbell rang, and when Truus opened the door, there stood three tired and dust-caked Americans with a little piece of paper saying that they had been billeted in the Zieren house for that night. The town's people had already been alerted by the mayor's office that the Americans would be housed with the citizens. Every house welcomed them with open arms. They were our honored guests. And they didn't come empty handed. They brought cigarettes and chocolate and some even took eggs with them. One thing was sure, they all needed a bath.

"I'm Andy," the corporal said. "This here is Joe and this is Charley."

They politely nodded their heads. They were members of the 78th Armored Field Artillery, a unit of the 2nd Armored Division, VII Corps, First Army.

"I'm Mr. Zieren. This is my daughter Truus, and this is Barth." Mr. Zieren introduced us in broken English. In Dutch fashion, he didn't mention his first name.

"Please sit down."

"Would you like something to eat or drink?" I asked.

184

We were still so stiff, so rusty, not used to suddenly speaking English.

"No, no." Andy put his hand up. "We ate, thank you. Thank you," he repeated to Truus.

"Here, this is for you."

All three went to their pockets and produced chocolate bars and chewing gum. Joe asked politely whether he could smoke.

"Yes, please, smoke," Mr. Zieren said. He handed Joe an ashtray.

"Would you gentlemen like a bath," Truus said.

"Yes Ma'am, please, yes." All three men said yes and please in unison and that broke the ice. We all had a good laugh and relaxed.

"Where shall we put them?" Truus said when they had left the room.

"One can go in my bed. I'll take the couch," I put in.

"Truus, you can sleep with me," Mr. Zieren said. "By the way, where is Joep?"

In all the excitement we hadn't noticed that Joep had disappeared and none of us knew where he had gone. The Americans stayed for two nights. Corporal Tarnik slept in my bed, Joe in Joep's bed, and Charlie slept in Truus' room. They were gone early next morning and returned late that evening with more food.

"Why didn't the Germans put you to work in Germany?" Andy asked me.

"I have a permit to work at the mine. It's called an Ausweis. This is what it looks like." I showed him my Ausweis.

"Well, Barth, if you ever come to the States, look me up," he said.

"Then you better give me your address." I laughed.

"Here, why don't you write it on the back of my Ausweis? I don't need it anymore. I'll keep it as a souvenir."

<hr>

185

Corporal Andy Tarnik's invitation to visit him in the States.

The division moved on the next morning, but one truck stayed behind. I couldn't see the driver—only two boots sticking out from under the truck, but I certainly had a fast lesson in the American way of swearing.

"You fucking son of a bitch. You lousy cocksucker. Goddamn piece of shit. What a fucking time to break down."

The man never stopped, not even when he appeared from under the truck and kicked a tire. An army tow truck arrived.

"What's wrong?" its driver said.

"I got a hole in the gear box. Sonuvabitch leaks oil faster than the tits of a cow."

The two men crawled under the truck and soon they formed a perfect duet. I was somewhat embarrassed by their swearing and yet fascinated by it. I was of the same age as those two soldiers, and despite having survived the occupation, I had lived a sheltered life compared to what they had gone through already. I had never before heard or read those words. "Fucking" and "cocksucker" were not exactly the kind of words I had learned from Miss Fijan, my English teacher in high school. We still read *Oliver Twist* and *The Scarlet Pimpernel*, and tried to understand works of Shakespeare.

186

The celebration of our newly found freedom lasted only one day. Then it was back to work in the mine, where we now worked hard to produce as much coal as possible. We didn't need any urging from the bosses. All of us knew that the people in the North were suffering. We were helping them to be warm that coming winter, when they too would be free. At least that's what we were thinking. I put in ten-hour days and was happy. The war was going well and soon I would be back with my family. Maybe back to medical school. In the meanwhile, Joep was still no where to be seen and Mr. Zieren was becoming concerned. But Truus wasn't worried about her brother.

"This isn't the first time he had been gone for some time. He'll show up again," she said.

When Corporal Tarnik and the others left Geleen, they didn't go very far. Their division stopped just ten miles north of town and dug in.

"Why aren't they moving on?" Mr. Zieren said.

"I don't know. Maybe they are waiting for reinforcement," I thought out loud.

But then the news came that British paratroopers had landed in Arnhem and that they had taken the bridge over the Rijn.

"It won't be long now and you can go back to Hilversum," Truus said.

"I'll keep my fingers crossed, but I have to see it first." I said with some reservation. Eindhoven hadn't even been taken and in order for the ground troops to reach Arnhem, they would have to fight their way across the Maas river, the wide Waal river and two canals, a distance of fifty miles and that seemed too big a bite to me. Four years of following the advances and retreats of the German army on our maps had taught me something about tactics and I didn't like it. Now it was also clear why the Americans had halted so soon after leaving Geleen. They protected the flank of the advancing

187

army as it battled through the narrow corridor. Eight days later, Montgomery had to admit defeat against the great rivers of Holland and I lost all hope of seeing my family soon.

After the Americans came the British, members of the Desert Rats Division. They taught me to play bridge and drink Scotch. And in December, elements of the U.S. Ninth Army took their place. Geleen had a special attraction for these soldiers, even for those who stopped only for a few hours. The modern mine Maurits was a clean mine and when the blackened miners returned above ground, they all took a shower to wash the coal dust away. The mine had a huge hall with numerous showerheads especially for that purpose. The soldiers came in truckloads, jumped off, and ran to see who would be the first to feel the warm water on their backs. God, did they make a lot of noise, but it was a happy noise. The news about the showers soon reached everywhere.

During the height of the Battle of the Bulge, the Germans advanced as far North as the outskirts of Spa, a town in Belgium only 24 miles South of Geleen. Wild rumors began to circulate. The wildest one concerned Otto Skorzeny, the notorious SS Colonel who, the previous year, had snatched Mussolini from the hotel in the Italian alps, where he had been imprisoned after his fall from power. Most of the rumors were just that—rumors. But one turned out to be true. English-speaking Germans in captured American uniforms had infiltrated deep behind the allied lines and were creating havoc in the rear areas. Hundreds of thousands of Americans were forced to play cat and mouse with each other when they met at crossroads or in the field. They no longer trusted passwords and relied on general knowledge like 'Who is the Yankee second baseman?'

One day, two American officers in a jeep drove up to the front gate of the mine and asked where the showers were. Even as far as twenty miles north of the battle, the American guard at the gate had orders to ask them a couple of questions.

"What is the capital of Ohio, captain?"

"Columbus." The captain smiled.

"What's the record for the most home runs in a season?"

"Sixty, and before you ask, it was Babe Ruth."

Again, it was the captain who answered. The lieutenant next to him looked straight ahead. The guard was satisfied. He saluted and waved them through.

While passing the time at the gate, the guard had been talking to one of my friends who had just come from work.

"There is something wrong about those two," my friend said.

"Oh yeah, what's that?"

"The other officer never said a word and I think I recognize an accent in that captain."

The guard hadn't noticed the accent, but the Dutchman had heard Germans talk for four years and he thought there was something odd.

"He said Rudth, not Ruth. He put a soft 'D' in it."

"Yeah. You know something, buddy, you're right. He did."

He called his sergeant and told him what my friend had said.

"You want to come with me?" the sergeant asked the Dutchman.

Together they went to the community shower and waited until the two officers in American uniforms stood naked.

"Who is the captain?" the sergeant said to my friend.

"The one with the blond hair."

The sergeant walked to the other officer.

"How is the water?" he said.

"The water is fine," the captain said immediately.

"I didn't ask you. You please keep quiet, sir."

The sergeant had his gun ready and pointed it at the second man.

189

"Now tell me, what outfit are you with?"

The man looked at his partner and shrugged his shoulders.

"Ich kann ja nicht antworten."

It was all over for the two gutsy Germans posing as American officers. They were about to pay the ultimate price. The sergeant motioned them to walk outside into the cold December winter. Much to our amusement, he then marched them, still wet and naked and shivering, to a jeep and drove off.

"What is going to happen with them?" I later asked an officer.

"They'll have a quick court-martial and be executed. Wearing the American uniform as a disguise means automatic death," he said nonchalantly.

January, 1945, was a cold month in Europe. At nine o'clock at night a jeep stopped in front of our house and the doorbell rang. When Truus opened the door, a tall, dark, uniformed figure told her that he had been billeted in her house. The man could hardly walk. He took his coat off and by a gold leaf on his shoulder, we realized that the newcomer was a major of the American armed forces.

Mr. Zieren put the major in his easy chair close to the stove and Truus made hot soup and coffee for him.

"I am with the Red Ball Express," he said, in beautiful English. "Have you heard of my outfit?"

"We sure have," I said. "It's called the life line of the army, isn't it?"

"Yes it is. I have just finished scouting the roads in Belgium and here. It was mighty cold in that open jeep. You'll soon see the Red Ball in action yourself."

When the other two Americans stationed in our house returned at ten o'clock, the one named Tex had a quick look at the major.

190

"It stinks in here," he said to his friend, a corporal.
"I smell it too," the corporal said. "Let's go upstairs. I can't stand that smell."

The officer said nothing and we didn't realize what was going on. The next day the major marked the roads with small yellow flags, from the corner of Main Street and Prins de Ligne Street, around the little circle in front of the church, and down the road leading to the mine.

The Red Ball Express rolled into town that evening. It was pitch dark, but the heavy trucks drove down our short street at an incredible speed, one right smack behind the other, rounding the circle as if the drivers had done it every day, and raced towards the mine. The only lights were thin slits in the headlamps. We only saw the whites of eyes and sometimes of teeth exposed in a grin. It was a fantastic display of driving. A ceaseless belt of trucks thundered by for hours. The major stayed with us for another day and when he left he gave Truus a large box of chocolate. He had been a quiet, reserved gentleman, a man of few words.

The other two soldiers had stayed away while the officer was in our house, but as soon as he left, they returned.

"Begging you pardon ma'am," the corporal said to Truus. "It isn't that we don't appreciate your hospitality. It was that nigger, ma'am. Can't stand them."

During the past two days, we had learned a thing or two about race relations in the American army, but we hadn't grown up with it and didn't understand the one sided hatred. We liked the major.

"The major is a fine gentleman," Truus said.

"But didn't you smell him, ma'am?" Tex said.

"No, we didn't." Truus became annoyed.

"Well, niggers stink. There is something in their skin or in the stuff they put in their hair that makes them stink." Tex tried to convince us, but we wouldn't buy it. From then on there was a chill between us.

191

Mr. Zieren at long last received word from Joep. He was in an American army hospital. On the day he disappeared, he volunteered as an interpreter for the Americans and had been wounded in the Battle of the Bulge. A grenade fragment had shattered his elbow and he was waiting for reconstructive surgery. "I won't be home for a while," the short letter had stated.

"Well, at least he is safe and he can't get into any more trouble," Mr. Zieren said, matter-of-fact and yet relieved.

"You never know with Joep." Truus cried and laughed at the same time.

Once again, we had a real newspaper and an announcement appeared in a February issue that a Dutch recruitment officer would come to town to give interviews. After four years of relative inactivity, it was no wonder that every able young man tried to sign up. I too went and when it was my turn to be interviewed, the officer asked about my schooling and my plans for the future. I mentioned that I had a grant to go to medical school.

"I don't think there'll be much money to give out grants for a while, and we don't know when the north will be free and the universities open again. It may take a while."

It was a sober and realistic appraisal of my situation.

"Without the grant, I can't go back to medical school."

The officer was sympathetic. I looked around the small room in which the interview took place. Behind the officer was a faded portrait of Queen Wilhelmina, the same portrait that hung in all official buildings before the war. They must have dug this one up from the archives, where it had been hidden for four years.

"I'll tell you what," he said. "The most immediate need of our army right now is new officers. I was lucky to be in England when the war broke out and know first hand that there are very few Dutch officers trained in modern warfare.

We need people like you. If I were in your place, I'd try to become an officer, serve a few years, and save the money I make to use for my study later."

The man made sense.

"Can I think it over?"

"Sure. I'll be here for two days. Let me know one way or another. Good luck."

Back home, I went upstairs to my room to think. Back home. Suddenly the thought of calling it home struck me as being funny. How many places had I called home? The thoughts about the future wouldn't come. I stared out of the window and didn't register what I saw. My brain drew nothing but blanks. Then I smiled. It wasn't a happy smile. I smiled because the first thought trying to fill the emptiness went back to the days with Bets and Ann, when my brain was empty at times. Then, too, I sat as I sat now.

"Well, what are you going to do?" I mumbled to myself. "You really don't want to be an officer, do you? But then what?"

No more thoughts, only emptiness again. With my hands behind the back of my head I lasted it out, waited until the thoughts returned.

"Okay, Barth, let's face the facts. You have to make a decision sooner or later. You can't talk it over with Mother and Dad, so you might as well make up your mind. You are only twenty years old and medical school can wait a few years longer. That study grant only pays for the tuition and all the other costs came from what your family scraped together. That must not happen again. Somehow or another you must come up with the money yourself. The officer showed you a way out. What's wrong with that?"

The longer I thought, the more sense it made to enter the army and so I decided. The next day, I saw the officer again.

"Sir, I want to enlist."

"Good. I'm glad you do. You won't be sorry."

193

In the first week of March, we new recruits reported to a captain and a sergeant in an office that had been vacated for their use by the Philips Electrical Company in Eindhoven. It took a few days before all volunteers reported, and those who arrived early were led to the second floor of a large building, where long rows of straw had been laid out for us to sleep. We were given food and a blanket and were on our own. There was nothing to do but wait and we went to sleep early.

I woke up in the middle of the night to find a woman with me under the blanket. A group of White Russians had arrived in the middle of the night and had temporarily been assigned to our floor. White Russia, also known as Byelorussia, was bordered to the West by Poland, to the South by the Ukraine, the North by the Baltic Sea and to the East by Russia. Its capital was Minsk. Centuries ago they were given the name White Russian, because the men wore traditional homespun white garments. The Germans had reduced their country to a virtual desert. They had completely destroyed all major cities, and groups of White Russians now wandered all over Europe. When the younger women in the group saw us sleeping under the blankets, they decided to seek warmth as well, and I couldn't blame them. It was cold outside, the straw gave little protection from the cement floor, and one army blanket wasn't enough to keep warm, even when we slept in our clothes. I must admit that I didn't mind sharing my blanket with that woman. Cuddled up, we were both warm.

The woman was still asleep when I woke up. She was about my age and not bad looking. An older woman came over and kicked her feet, which made her sit up. She smiled at me and the good looks made place for an ugly set of teeth with two gaping holes. The White Russians were a strange bunch, about a hundred of them. Stocky women did all the work, while their men sat around and smoked. When they were ready to leave, the women carried heavy bundles of their belongings on their backs and head, and the men walked behind, carrying only a little cane. They did give us a present—lice. We were ordered to throw the straw out of the window to be burned, and then we were deloused. Members of a British medical team lined us up and one by one we underwent the DDT treatment. A corporal sprayed my hair, my armpits, and then stuck the nozzle of his spray can in my pants. We were told not to take a bath for forty-eight hours, which was no great deal, because there were no showers anyway.

On March 27th, early in the morning of our third day in Eindhoven, several army trucks arrived. We were allowed to take one piece of luggage and some fellows complained that wasn't enough to pack all their stuff. I wore the only clothes I had and carried my belongings, consisting of a razor, toothbrush, and comb in my pocket.

"You're traveling mighty light, mate," the driver of the truck said.

I was on my way to England.

15

The Homecomings

On September 5, 1946, after eighteen months in England, I returned to Hilversum, to my parents. I walked around to the back door, through the kitchen, and opened the door to the living room. Dad was alone in the room, reading the newspaper in his easy chair next to the stove. He looked up. He wore spectacles. He hadn't worn them when I saw him last, but that was more than four years ago. Otherwise, he looked exactly the same—the hair unruly with some gray creeping in on the sides, a wide smile exposed the same yellow teeth and three fingers were covered with black tape.

"Well I'll be darned, doggone it, I'll be darned," he said.

We looked at each other affectionately.

"I brought you something," I said and gave him a long narrow package.

"Thanks, but you should have saved your money. I got all I need."

The man didn't own a thing, other than an old, single barrel shotgun, a dog, and a couple of tame ducks. Ten years ago, the butt of the gun, long split from old age had finally broken and from a piece of three by two he had carved a new one with his pocketknife. He unwrapped the package and out came a beautiful, double-barreled shotgun I had bought in Scotland. His hard-worked hands caressed the carvings on the butt as if it was a newborn baby. He stroked the barrels, shouldered the gun, and looked down the sights. The end of

EYES OF THE BLIND

the butt, which was partially hollowed out to hold two cartridges, had a cover made of ivory. Its carving showed a hunter and his dog. Dad had trouble clearing his throat.

"I'll give my single barrel to Jan Rempe."

He got out of his chair and we embraced. It was good to feel the stubble of his beard on my cheek.

"Mother is in the front room," he said.

Mother was in bed, where she had been for the past two years. She held her arms out and we hugged and in the hug I felt how weak she was.

"Welcome home, son."

"It's good to be home, Mom."

Neither of us could say more. She had lost a lot of weight. The muscles in her arms and hands were for the most part wasted, and there were unhealthy blushes on her pale cheeks. The room needed fresh air.

"I brought you a present."

She had trouble taking the string off and I gave her a hand. Out came a woolen shawl, also from Scotland, where I had last been stationed. She put it around her shoulders.

"Now I can keep warm." She gave me another hug.

"You rest now, Mom. I'll be back."

"No, I also have a surprise." She didn't say what it was.

"Why don't you and I go and have a drink?" I suggested to Dad, when I returned to the family room. I had to get out of the house and could use a drink. "You know, get the dust out of our throats."

Dad smiled. "Good idea."

We walked to the pub one block over and Dad showed off his son in the British officer's dress uniform. I bought a round, and the owner of the pub bought a round, and Dad bought a round. And we both felt a lot better and went home, the real home. Dad returned to the new gun and I looked around. The door slowly opened and step after careful step, while holding on to the wall with both hands, Mother shuffled

197

HOOG

in. Dad and I both rushed to help her, but she waved us off. I quickly emptied the other armchair next to the stove and we eased her in.

"Phew," she puffed triumphantly.

The backdoor flew open and Coos stormed in.

"Oh boy, you're back." She hugged and kissed me like I was her boyfriend. Then, over my shoulder, she saw Mother.

"Well lookie there, a double surprise." She turned to me. "See, all you have to do is show up and she's better. Here, let me make some tea. We have real tea now, you know."

She started fussing all over us. Brother Jaap came home at six. He looked like a grown man now.

"Hi, about time you showed up."

"Good to see you again, baby brother."

We had the hardest handshake imaginable. Then I gave them the bad news.

"I have only one week leave and then I have to report for duty in Assen. Three weeks from now, we board ship for Indonesia."

They fell silent.

"Well, let's make the best of it." It was typically Coos, her chin up.

After dinner, their stories filled me in about the past three years.

Mr. Loopstra had witnessed the raid from his front window. After the Germans left, he went over to Bets and Ann and later he and Bets went to tell my parents what had happened. Mrs. Sterk, or rather Mrs. Stern, didn't have a chance. They found her hiding under her bed in the attic and pushed her none too softly down the stairs and into the waiting truck. She was transported to the notorious concentration camp Westerdorp, where she spent the rest of the war. They found my papers, some underwear, and socks in my bedroom and questioned the two sisters about it. Bets and Ann put on their best blind act, and Bets especially kept her cool.

"That belongs to Ernst. He is a blind student who has been living with us. But he isn't here today."

"That doesn't explain this identity card," the officer, who did the interrogating, persisted.

"Did he forget them again? He always forgets something." Ann came up with that reply.

The officer may have had his doubts about that, but he was evidently satisfied having found Mrs. Stern.

"You people were hiding a Jew."

"She is our maid," Bets objected. "We weren't hiding her. How could we know that she is a Jew?"

"She just worked here. We are blind, don't you see?" Ann added.

Even the German could appreciate that logic. A soldier came into the hallway with the large map. He gave it to the officer. Pins rattled on the parquet floor.

"What are you doing with a map if you are blind?"

"That doesn't mean that we can't feel. We like to follow the progress of the victorious German army."

Even at that moment Bets couldn't resist, but her sarcasm didn't penetrate the thick German skulls. In the end they left without arresting the sisters.

A week later, my parents were visited by a police detective, an old-timer, who knew them well. One could call it a friendly get-together and Mother would have served tea, but there was no longer any tea to serve. And Mother was too weak to get up from the couch that had been transformed into a bed.

"Gijs, I'm sorry, but I have to ask you some questions."

"That's all right, Wim. Go ahead."

"When did you last see your son? Bartholomeus is his first name isn't it?"

"That's easy. Barth left for Germany on the day that the students had to report for deportation."

"Are you sure he left?"

"Sure I'm sure. Asked our neighbors. They saw him leave."

"He never arrived in Germany. Did you know that?"

"Well I'll be darned. Mother, did you hear that? Barth isn't in Germany."

"I heard. Wim, do you know where he is?"

"No, Ali, but we have a good idea where he was all this time."

"Then you know more than we do." Mother was as cool as a cucumber.

"Didn't he used to drive that blind music teacher back and forth to the Institute for the Blind?"

The detective remained friendly. His was not an easy job during the war years. The mayor and the police chief were both Nazis, as were the newcomers to the police force. Together, they had put the squeeze on the old-timers.

"A week ago, there was a raid on her house and they found some man's clothing. According to a Jewish woman, who was picked up during the raid, the clothes belonged to a nephew, but the real nephew lives in Amsterdam and he didn't know anything about those clothes. We now think that they may have belonged to your son."

"You got to believe me, Wim," Dad said with a straight face. "We never knew that. But then they didn't catch him, did they?"

"No they didn't. And you don't know where he is, do you?"

"No we don't. I sure wish we did, though."

The interrogation ended at that point and they talked a while longer about the times before the war. The detective left with some friendly advice for Dad.

"You be careful, Gijs. This may not be the end of it."

And it wasn't. On August 12, a barber named Piet van Ettekoven, one of the lesser German sympathizers, warned Dad while he was giving him a haircut.

"Gijs, I'm not supposed to tell you, but there is a rumor that they'll come for you one of these days."

"I'll be waiting. I got nothing to tell them, but thank you anyway, Piet."

That same evening, my parents' house was surrounded by the Germans, the Dutch police, and by a Nazi called Vennekool. He used to be one of Dad's plasterers, but he had a bad work attitude and Dad had fired him soon after they began work on the villas on Chestnut Street. After the Germans overran Holland, he showed up in a Nazi uniform and became one of the most feared Quislings in Hilversum. Searchlights went on and they turned the house inside out. In the meanwhile, Vennekool, with hatred in his eyes, interrogated Dad. Mother was in the hospital suffering from severe malnutrition.

"Your son never reported for transportation to Germany and you know damn well where he's hiding."

"What do you mean he didn't report? He left here on his way to Utrecht to report. You can ask the neighbors. They saw him leave."

Dad repeated the part about the neighbors, because one of them was a known Nazi. He had important witnesses. Vennekool grabbed Dad by his collar, shoved him against the wall, and pushed his chin up with the barrel of his gun.

"God dammit, you lying bastard. You know damn well that he was with those blind music teachers. The Jew bitch told us all about it. Now where the hell is he?"

Dad, normally a short-tempered man, remained ice calm. He knew that if he made one wrong move, Vennekool would let him have it.

"I don't know where he is and if I knew I wouldn't tell you."

201

Vennekool spat Dad in the face. "I ought to kill you right now."

A senior police officer interfered.

"Take it easy, Vennekool. He probably doesn't know. Why don't we take him to headquarters where we can interrogate him better?"

Actually, Dad told the truth. He didn't know where I was. While this was going on, the Germans ransacked the house, but didn't find anything. Their commander had seen enough.

"Last mal gehen," he ordered, "Let's go."

They left and led Dad through a line of curious neighbors. Dad soon noticed a change in attitude amongst the Germans. They teased the corporal about something and laughed amongst themselves. It was as if they were glad that their job was finished for the night. Dad also observed that none of the police officers were young recruits. He knew several of them from before the war and sensed that they were friendly to him. They, in turn, knew him to be an old Hilversummer, who had married the daughter of Bart Knegt, the Erfgooier. It counted. Dad decided to take a chance and refused to walk further.

"If you're going to shoot me, you might as well get it over with right now," he bluffed. He ripped his shirt open and stuck his chest out.

Vennekool wanted to keep going to the police station, but the police hated him and even the Germans despised him. After some arguing, they decided to let Dad go. And go Dad did, running like a rabbit in the open field, with sudden moves to the left and right, waiting for a bullet to hit. "You can go" was used as a favorite tactic to shoot a prisoner in the back with the excuse that he was trying to escape. No bullet came. Dad told Mother what had happened when he visited her in the hospital the next day.

"What do you think will happen to him?" she asked.

"Don't worry about Barth; he can take care of himself. They didn't catch him, did they? He'll make it, you'll see." Together, they sat in the quiet of the hospital, unsure what the future would bring.

A bed came free in my parents' house when I left and, unbeknown to me, Frans had moved over from the crowded house on 84 Egelantierstraat to my parent's house. It was a small world. When Frans learned of his father's arrest, he left to search for him. Mr. Smale and my parents had tried to talk him out of it.

"Your dad can be in any of the concentration camps by now," Mother had argued. "He may already be in Germany."

But it was no use.

"I have to find him," he said and left into the night.

It was as if his mind had shut out everything else, as if he was following a destiny.

"So, when Mr. Loopstra came to warn you Frans wasn't even with the Smales."

"That's right, he was already here," Mother smiled.

"But then what happened with him when the Germans raided your house?"

"When I was warned by van Ettekoven, we moved Frans a few houses down for a few days," said Dad. He said it as if it was nothing, something you do every day. How little did I know what happened outside my own hiding place during those years.

"That reminds me. What happened to Doctor Zwaap?"

"He, his wife and children all died in the concentration camp."

"I'm sorry to hear that."

Mother also told how she had become involved with the delivery of food ration coupons to houses where people were underground. In late 1943, a man from the distribution office came to the house.

"Mrs. Hoogstraten, are you paying for extra ration coupons?"

"Who are you and why are you asking?" Mother was cautious, even though she recognized the man as the son of an Erfgooier.

"I am from the distribution bureau and it is my understanding that you need extra rations," the man said.

"Do I look like I get extra rations?" asked mother with sarcasm.

"Yes, you certainly do, but believe me I know you're getting them."

He didn't explain how he knew. The man looked convincing, not at all like an overconfident, brash Dutch Nazi. But one could never tell and Mother remained cautious.

"I don't know what you're talking and thank you to leave my house," she said with a straight face.

The man looked at her and smiled. "I understand. But please, when someone asks for payment, do not pay. They are free." He left.

He returned three weeks later with a request for Mother to go to a restaurant on the Damrak in Amsterdam, a busy street close to the railroad station.

"I'd like you to pick up some books for me."

"Just plain, regular books?" Mother said. She had decided to trust the man.

"Would I be asking you if it weren't plain, regular books?" The man held Mother's eyes.

The next morning, she went to Amsterdam by train, sat down at a table in the designated restaurant, and ordered a glass of lemonade. After about ten minutes, a man carrying three books tied with a string under his arms joined her. He placed the books on the table between them and ordered a cup of imitation coffee, the only coffee available. They talked as if they had known each other for a long time and when the man left, the books remained on the table. Mother finished her lemonade, got up and walked back to the station, three books under her arm.

The man from the distribution office returned in the evening and Mother gave him the books. Mother had become a courier for the underground as so many other women did during the war when their men could no longer walk the streets. Mother made two more trips to Amsterdam and then the man asked her to do something else.

"We don't want the same person to make too many trips. If I give you a few addresses, could you drop these envelopes off? All you have to do is put them in the mail slot."

There were no mailboxes in Holland. All mail and newspapers were delivered through a slot in the front door.

"I'll see to it," Mother replied.

From then on Mother and brother Jaap delivered the envelopes, the kind that were dropped off at the house of the sisters Frank once a month. They contained food coupons.

"Why did that man come to see you? How did he know that you could be trusted? And how did you know that you could trust him?" I said.

"I don't know the answers to those first two questions," she said. "But I do know his family. They are Erfgooiers and I trust them."

There it was again. Old Hilversummers and the Erfgooiers.

"And come to think of it, he may have known that my father was an Erfgooier," she added.

On my second day back, I rang the doorbell of 35 Rembrandt Avenue and a strange woman answered. She frowned when she saw me in that uniform.

"Yes?"

"How do you do? You must be the new help. Are Bets and Ann in?"

For a moment, she was puzzled and then she smiled.

"You must be looking for the ladies Frank. They don't live here anymore."

She didn't know where they had moved to, but mentioned that Ann had married. It was disappointing not to see them again. Ann must have married Mr. Zieren, I thought.

I called on Nienke and was she ever surprised to see me in that splendid dress uniform, complete with shiny leather belt and cane. Quite a difference from the brown pants and green velvet jacket. I felt pretty confident. My heart jumped when I saw her. She hadn't changed and the love that hadn't died came back to me as never before. We went for a walk on the heather with her dog Prent.

"That uniform looks good on you," she said.

I told her what had happened to me in the last four years and she did the same.

"You know we had several raids while you were away," she said.

"I know of only one." I told her about the night when the Germans walked by on their socks. "So that's why we didn't hear them coming, the sneaks," she exclaimed. "Miek saw them first when she woke up and opened the window. There was a soldier standing on top of our bicycle shed and she yelled, "Ist die Invasion schon da?" (Did the invasion take place)? Crazy Miek isn't scared of anything. There were also soldiers in the street and they searched all houses. The one who came to our house said that he was from Austria. To our surprise, he actually apologized for the inconvenience. Can you imagine? He only looked briefly into each room and missed my nephew, who was hiding in a space above a closet. He said that he was not supposed to leave without taking something."

Nienke suddenly started to laugh.

"What's the matter, why are you laughing?"

206

"Do you know what he left with? Mother gave him a wash cloth and I still see him walking away with it. He was really a nice man. Unfortunately, they did round up two Jews and arrested the owners of the houses in which they were hidden."

"You know, you mentioned that he missed your nephew, who was hidden in the space above a closet. Let me tell you what we did with the closet."

We walked back as I told the story about Mrs. Sterk being stuck in the closet. At the door she shook my hand.

"Thank you for coming by and filling me in," she said.

"Thank you too."

We shook hands. That was all. I hadn't dared to tell her that I loved her without a sign of encouragement, and there had been none. Three weeks later, I was on the boat to Indonesia.

On January 15, 1947, she sent me a letter. I know the date, because in my diary, I entered the dates of all letters from Holland, from family and friends. She wrote at irregular intervals and I saved all her letters. One time I felt so strongly that her letter would come that it made me restless. And a letter came. That happened twice and from then on, it almost became a routine. I felt it coming and it came. In July there were three letters. That was the month Mother went to her house to say that I had been seriously wounded in battle and placed on the danger list. They were letters of encouragement and she enclosed a photo of herself in the snow. I kept the photo on my nightstand and when our division commander, General Durst-Britt, came visiting with his favorite niece at his side, he asked:

"Is that your girl?"

"No, general, but I sure hope so one day."

"Well, good luck to you."

Three months later I was back in the field. On June 8, 1949, our troopship approached the coast of Holland at night and we were all on deck looking at the lights. Her last letter was handed to me at two o'clock that night, when our ship moved slowly through the locks of IJmuiden. We were back in Holland and eager to leave the ship, but first had to endure a long speech from the Minister of War, the playing of the national anthem, a welcome word from the Commander in Chief and other niceties from important people, who were all too dumb to realize that soldiers didn't want to hear any speeches. We had just wasted several years of our lives and we were eager to go home.

At noon, I finally boarded a bus and two hours later it turned into Egelantier Street. There were flags everywhere and a huge banner, hung across the street, read "Welcome Home." People came pouring into the street. As the bus slowly made its way through the crowd, a woman ran ahead and rang our doorbell.

"Ali! Gijs! He is here!"

By the time I stepped from the bus, Mother had somehow managed to be at the foot of the steps. A big, wet kiss on both cheeks and she wouldn't let go of me. Held on to me for dear life. Dad smiled from ear to ear and used his handkerchief to wipe a tear away. Hankies are for eyes, I remembered. The house was packed with people. Even my buddy Jan van Elderen, who had been my neighbor for eight weeks in the hospital, had traveled from his home in Eindhoven to welcome me. It was too much, too many people.

"We want to show you something."

Mam and Dad walked hand in hand in the narrow corridor to the front room, all six steps. They opened the door and pride shone in their eyes when they let me in. There it was—the old table, the chair, and a bookcase. And the microscope in the case on the floor next to the table. But the big surprise came when Mother turned on a real, honest to goodness desk lamp. Earlier that year, the housing association had at long last put electricity in the front rooms of all houses in our street.

"You are all set to go back to your study," Dad said.

"Back to medical school," Mother beamed.

Now I needed a handkerchief. Seven years had passed since I first entered med school. At eight-thirty, the doorbell rang. I opened the door, and there she was with a big smile. Nienke gave me a little hug and suddenly it dawned on me that she was shy. I took her as far as the door to the living room. "We're going for a walk." I waved.

16

The Storm and the Sisters Revisited

I had indeed saved nearly all my pay, as the recruitment officer in Geleen had told me I could, only he had been wrong about the duration of my time in the service. The couple of years had turned into nearly five years. I now had money to burn in my pocket. I took Nienke sailing, to dinner, to a show, and on the fourteenth day, asked her to become my wife.

"Yes, I'll marry you," she said. "On one condition. We must leave Holland."

She wanted to see more of the world. After experiencing the wide world, I also had the feeling that our country was too small for me to spend the rest of my life in and I readily agreed. "Do you love me?" I asked.

"I respect you from that day in class, when you spoke up against De Wijn and Wolters."

I remembered how she had turned around that day in class and had smiled at me. She was now twenty-six years old and it was time to pick her mate for life. It was love the Friesian way, the way her father had described. She took the grandson of an Erfgooier. Ten days later, she gave me the first kiss, and a year later we exchanged engagement rings. She continued to work in Amsterdam. I went to med school in Utrecht and we both lived in Hilversum.

The recruitment officer had also been wrong about the study grant. They were made available soon after the war ended—something I found out after my return from Java. And I found out something else. The students who had signed the loyalty declaration to the Germans were now nearly finished with their study and two of them were my instructors. There was another surprise waiting. I was taking tennis lessons and the pro encouraged me to participate in a tournament. I beat an older man in the first round and when I showed up the next morning for the second round, of all people in the world, Jan de Wijn, the former leader of the Nazi youth movement in our high school, walked on the court.

That was too much. He was back in the graces of Hilversum. I left to see the tournament director.

"Look, my opponent is a former Nazi and he went with the Dutch Legion to the Russian front. I can't play with him."

"Well sir, Mr. de Wijn has been cleared of everything and he is a member of the club. I am afraid I can't make an exception. He is your opponent."

I was not a member of the club.

"You mean to say that I, who went to England to fight on our side, am now forced to play with a traitor who fought on the German side?" I was getting angry.

"I'm sorry sir, but that's the way it'll have to be."

That was the end of the tournament for me. De Wijn had a walkover.

I had to give him credit though for following his principles. He did go to the Russian front and he never committed a crime against the Dutch, unlike Wolters, who started a campaign of terror in Hilversum. He and van Drie were caught and condemned to several years in prison.

In September 1952, Nienke had a surprise for me when I saw her at her home.

211

"Why don't we get married?"

"Get married?" I was flabbergasted. "What brought that up so suddenly?"

We were supposed to get married when I finished med school, which was in another two years.

"A friend at work said that we were crazy. We both live in Hilversum, you go to Utrecht, and I go to Amsterdam for work. We can rent an apartment from the money we save on train costs."

It made sense.

"If we do it, we better be fast, because med school in Amsterdam starts again in two weeks."

"So?" she said.

"So we get married."

Thirteen days later, we were married in the beautiful, completely restored town hall, and rented two rooms from Mrs. Spruit, who lived on the third floor of an apartment building on the Amstelkade in Amsterdam.

"I have fixed the bed myself," she said proudly. "And I had a wash basin installed in the bedroom. We can share the kitchen."

The bed collapsed in the middle of the night.

"What will the neighbors downstairs think?" Nienke said.

"Who cares." We burst out laughing.

While I went to med school, she worked and earned our living. Only once did she ask me to keep an eye on something that was cooking in the kitchen while she was away.

"I have soup bones on a slow boil. Can you remember to turn off the gas in forty-five minutes?"

"What do you mean, can you remember? Of course I can."

She left and I studied in the living room and forgot. When, after several hours, I finally looked up from the books, there hung a blue haze in the room. The hallway was cloudy, the kitchen black. I opened the window and huge clouds escaped in a hurry. My hand searched for the knob of the gas stove. I was smart enough to take a wet towel in my hands before picking up the pan. A howl of laughter went up from the women in the apartments behind us, who, curious about the black clouds, saw me appear with the pan filled with pitch-black bones. Tar drops hung from the ceiling in the kitchen and from the lamp in the hallway. I spent the rest of the day cleaning, but couldn't get rid of the smell.

"What happened?" Nienke asked when she came home. I had to relate the whole sorry story. It was the last time she asked me to do something in the kitchen.

On Saturday afternoon, January 31, 1953, Nienke and I were walking on the ring dike around the Aalsmeer polder, about ten miles Southeast of Amsterdam. A cold, blustery Northwestern bit in our faces and forced us to lean forward. Nienke stayed half a step behind me so that I could act as her windbreaker. The storm bowed the crowns of the poplar trees that lined the entire length of the dike and down below it flattened the grass of some of the richest grazing land in the world.

"That's one heck of a storm," I yelled, but the words flew by Nienke before she could hear them. "I sure wouldn't like to be at sea right now."

She tried to smile, but the force of the wind contorted her face into a grimace as if she were in pain. Little did we know that the North Sea was probably one of the safer places to be that weekend. We returned to our bikes where we had left them at a gate, but it was no use trying to ride because the wind would blow us over. The wind continued to increase in force and turned into one the worst storms ever to hit the coast of Holland. When it was over, I decided to tell Bets and Ann about it.

"I'm going to pay a visit to the sisters," I told Nienke. "They know only of the storm by what they heard on the radio and I can give them a much better picture."

"Yes, do that," she said.

I had learned that the sisters now lived two miles outside Hilversum, a short train ride from Amsterdam. I could hear piano music in the background when I rang the doorbell. Bets opened the door.

"Hello Bets."

Her whole face lightened up when she recognized my voice.

"Barth, so nice to see you."

They still said 'see'.

She took me into the living room where Ann was playing.

"We have a visitor," said Bets.

"Who is it," asked Ann in a neutral voice.

I walked over to her and took her hand.

"It's Barth," she said happily, without needing to hear my voice. "What brings you here?"

"Well, I'm thirsty. Can you still make tea?"

They laughed.

"I'll make it," said Bets and she left for the kitchen.

"You know I married Cor Zieren," said Ann.

"I figured you might. What happened?"

"He died," she said, showing no emotion. "Back together with Bets. It's better that way."

I gave Bets a hand bringing in the tea when it was ready.

"I remember how amazed I was the first time I saw you handle that hot water, Bets. I thought you were going to burn your fingers for sure. But now I know better."

"I told you that we are normal people, didn't I?" she smiled.

"You sure did and I learned fast."

We returned to the living room and sat at the familiar round table, Ann in her chair on the right, Bets in hers on the left and I faced them.

"Well, let me tell you why I really came to see you. You've

———

heard about the storm on the radio and I thought you would like to hear something about it first hand from me."

Their faces brightened.

"That'll be real nice," said Bets. "Then I can see it better."

"From what we heard on the radio it must have been terrible," Ann said.

"It was. Let me begin by explaining why this became such a bad storm. During the last days of January, hurricane force winds whipped the waters of the Atlantic Ocean around the coast of Scotland and pushed an extra fifteen billion gallons of water down the North Sea. At the same time, the sun and moon worked together to create one of the highest tides the coast of Northern Europe had ever experienced. The English Channel was not wide enough to handle that gigantic mass of water, and it began to back up into the sea arms that separate the islands of Zeeland and South Holland. Soon the water breached the crown of the dikes and ate away at the back of the dikes. They broke through in several places and the water flooded the polders, the low-lying land the Dutch had reclaimed from the sea. At its deepest penetration, the floodwaters reached sixty-two miles inland at a point where the Netherlands is only one hundred miles wide.

As you know, about forty percent of Holland lies below sea level, some parts as much as twenty-five feet below. Canals and rivers form rings around the land that once formed the bottom of the sea, and it is not unusual for a farmer, working his fields down below, to see a ship go by high above his head. The Dutch began claiming land from the sea in the seventh century and by 1953 had taken some 1.8 million acres. Ninety percent of the land of two provinces—North and South Holland—lies below sea level, nearly all of Zeeland.

Formidable dunes that can withstand even the worst possible storm protected the coast of North Holland. South Holland also has dunes, but wide sea arms surround the two islands in Southern part of that province and only dikes gave

215

protection against high water. Zeeland, the country's most Southwestern province, is particularly vulnerable to floods. It consists of six islands, separated by sea arms that are up to seven miles wide in some places. The radio announcer said something about the strength of the storm and that it was high tide that day, but most Dutchmen paid little attention. They grew up with wind, water, and tides and weren't worried. The dikes would hold.

The wind howled throughout the night and the next day, Sunday, the news became real bad. At ten o'clock in the morning, the radio interrupted its regular program with a report that a flood had breached a dike in South Holland and that a man had drowned during the night. In the afternoon, eight more deaths were reported and in the early evening, the number jumped to fifty-eight. From then on, all normal radio programs were canceled and reports of a major disaster in Zeeland and South Holland filled the airways. From city halls in Zeeland, from police stations throughout the Southwest, from the Red Cross, and from lonely amateur radio operators in flooded villages came requests for help. The rest of Holland held its breath.

When I went to class at the University of Amsterdam on Monday morning, I learned that the student body had hired two tour busses and was anxious to leave for the flood area. However, a police officer had ordered the drivers to keep the bus doors locked, because the authorities had blocked all roads leading South. A motley bunch of students milled around the busses. They wore rain gear, jack-boots, riding boots, jodhpurs and colorful sweaters. Their headgear included caps, ski masks and even a Homburg. One red-faced, heavyset fellow wore tennis shoes. He hadn't bothered with a winter coat. They had brought shovels, picks, axes, and the wiser ones had blankets. Female students eager to lend a hand made sandwiches and filled thermos bottles with hot coffee. The

EYES OF THE BLIND

students protested angrily that they had a right to go, but it was no use fighting the cop.

"Why don't we try to get permission from the military?" I said.

My suggestion was received without much enthusiasm.

"And how do you figure to do that?" a self appointed leader of the group said sarcastically.

"We can try, can't we?"

I jumped on my bike and went back home. Nienke was just about to leave for work.

"Why did you come back?" she asked.

"Nobody is going to lectures. The students are in an uproar. They want to go to Zeeland to help, but the police won't let them leave."

"It's bad, isn't it? What are you going to do?"

"I'm going to see whether I can get them to go."

I put my officer's uniform on and kissed Nienke good bye.

"I doubt that I'll be able to get in touch with you for a while."

I took my hip boots, a leftover from before the war and biked back to the university. At the busses, the students were still mingling without much hope.

"Officer, I have received orders to take these students to Walcheren."

The police officer looked at my uniform and shook his head in doubt. But he smiled knowingly and winked. "You're sure you received those orders, sir?"

"I sure did," I replied with a straight face.

"Well, in that case it's okay with me. You can get in, gentlemen."

Police officers in university towns addressed students as gentlemen, at least at that time. We were off to Zeeland, "Land of the Sea", an ominous name indeed. Military police halted our busses in Breda.

"Sorry, sir. No one is allowed to go through. From here on all roads are blocked." The sergeant was adamant.

Behind me the students suddenly became very quiet.

"I told you so," one whispered.

"Blocked to where, sergeant?" I said.

"To the West, sir, to Roosendaal and beyond."

Nearly all roads leading to Zeeland went via Roosendaal. But I was ready for his reply.

"We aren't going West, sergeant. We're going to Antwerp."

He looked at me, looked at the anxious faces of the students behind me and made up his mind.

"Antwerp? My orders say nothing about Antwerp. As far as I'm concerned, you can go."

He wished us good luck and waved us on.

"What the hell are we going to Antwerp for?" The fellow with the tennis shoes wanted to know.

"The roads going North from Antwerp lead to Zeeland, don't they?" I said.

The mood of the students changed abruptly. They sang one student song after another, some of them so rowdy that even the bus driver shook his head in disbelief. "You gentlemen sure use some strong language," he laughed as we sang praise to the lips, the breasts, and the loins of that beautiful maiden, just as we had in my little study room eight years ago.

A sympathetic Belgian border guard saluted and let us through without questions. He warned us that in Antwerp the tunnel under the Schelde might still be closed. When we arrived, the tunnel was under water, but an attendant at the entrance was willing to let us have a go at it. Slowly, one driver took his bus down the decline into the water, while his partner watched. At the deepest point, the water reached up to the axles, but the exhaust stayed just above the surface and he got through. Our vehicles were the first to make it.

After another hour, we arrived in Breskens, where a ferry took us across the four-mile wide sea arm to the island of Walcheren. In Middelburg, the capital city of Zeeland, we were welcomed with open arms. We were the first ones from the outside world to come to help. The chief engineer of dikes on the island directed us to the break in the main dike, northeast of Middelburg. If we could hold that gap to its present size or maybe even make it smaller, the engineers would be able to save the large pumping stations. Closing the gap was out of the question. There was some grumbling amongst the students.

"We came to save lives, not to fill sand bags." It was the heavyset fellow in the tennis shoes. Without a coat, he was already shivering in the cold wind, which, in that flat countryside, blew three, four times as hard as on the square in front of the university building in Amsterdam, something he evidently hadn't reckoned with.

"Yah, we didn't come all this way to work on a dike," the skinny youth standing next to him piped in a high pitched voice, his face blue from the cold. There was something funny about those two.

"Who the hell are you? Hey, anybody know these guys?" The students questioned them and soon found out that the skinny one was a girl. Neither she nor her fellow turned out to be students. Posturing as students, they had come along for the excitement. We sent them on their way and the busses took the rest of us over the dike in the direction of the break. The drivers, used to easy going on highways, picked their way carefully over the slippery dike. Two hundred yards from the point where the sea had broken through, they stopped and we walked the rest of the way. The gap was about forty feet wide and there was no telling how deep it was. It was high tide and the sea rushed in with tremendous force. There was water all around us as far as our eyes could see. A country road, its surface under water, led from the dike to a lonely

219

farm four hundred yards inland. A narrow strip of land behind the dike was the only place where we would be able to fill sandbags. No one said a word. The tremendous force of the wind, the turbulent water, the wide expanse, the hopelessness of it all left us speechless. We felt very lonely.

"We might as well start. We can't stand here forever," one of the students finally said. We walked back to the busses and began to fill sandbags. Thousands and thousands of bags we filled with the heavy clay. There were no heroics, just hard work, exposed to the cold and the wind, on top of a narrow dike with water on both sides. It was backbreaking work for students used to the easy life. Sad news drove us on—394 dead in the afternoon, 605 at midnight. We worked through the night and stopped only to eat the sandwiches and drink the coffee, which by now was lukewarm. By noon of the next day, we had a huge pile of sandbags waiting for the tide to shift. When the rush water slowed down, we threw the bags in the breach as fast as possible, but the sea took them away just as fast.

"This is useless," a student said.

"The bags just disappear like there's no bottom," another said.

'What do you think?" the student standing next to me asked. "You brought us here."

I had been thinking while they were talking.

"Our only hope is that a couple of bags will eventually reach bottom and stay put. Maybe twenty, thirty feet away from here. If we throw fast enough, other bags might stick behind them and start building a ridge."

He mulled it over. "You mean forming a tongue of sand bags?"

"Yes, and when that tongue builds up, the root of the tongue eventually may reach the surface."

It seemed a crazy idea, but it was the only one I had.

"Well, we might as well try," the student said. "Hey you guys, listen."

He explained the plan and we went back to work. It happened. A loud cheer went up when the first bags no longer disappeared in the deep. From then on we were possessed with new enthusiasm. The tongue of bags began to extend into the breach and slowly, ever so slowly, the gap became smaller. When the tide water rushed back in again with full force, we stopped and looked. The break was only twenty feet wide.

By late afternoon, the students, not used to hard physical labor, were close to exhaustion. They badly needed a warm meal and a good night's sleep; otherwise, they wouldn't be of much use the next day. I sent one of the busses back for food and hot drinks and walked down the narrow, unpaved road in the direction of the farm, looking for a place to sleep that night. I walked in a strange silence. No dog barked, no cow mooed. No sound.

The farm buildings were surrounded by water. The front door and one of the windows of the farmhouse stood open, evidence that the owners had left in a hurry. Water rippled back and forth across the windowsill. The curtain waved with the flow. A large wooden chest had toppled and floated on top of the water. The table hit against it. A piece of carpet sloshed back and forth. Wading hip high through the water, I made my way through the front door, where pots and pans drifting aimlessly met me. One of the pans had a passenger—a doll. Its arms dangled over the side as if it was playing with the water. A little girl must have used the pan as a boat for her doll while waiting to be evacuated. Upstairs, the beds were neatly made. A proud farmer's wife couldn't possibly leave without the beds being made.

Outside, where the yard had been, drowned chickens drifted against the side of the barn. I entered through a small door in one of the huge barn doors. An eerie silence met me. My eyes got used to the dim light and then I saw it.

The farmer, unable to take his cows with him, had built a mountain of straw bales. When it reached high up in the barn, he had used other bales to make steps that led to the top of the mountain. He had driven his cows up the steps, one by one, and he had tied them to the huge center beam, all neatly in a row. When he left, he must have taken a last look and thought that at least they were safe up there, high in the barn, on top of the bales. Only the water had come higher than he thought possible, and the bales on the bottom came loose and began drifting away. First the steps, then the base of the mountain crumbled, until there was no mountain left.

The cows hung from the center beam, necks stretched under the weight of heavy bodies, wild eyes bulging, tongues hanging from wide-open mouths. Noses dried with foam. Abdomens sagged low, forming grossly distended balloons. In their agony, the cows had started to kick and their sharp hooves ripped open the swollen udders of their neighbors, pieces hanging in tatters. Milk had changed the water below into a dirty white pool. Blood had dripped, clotting as it went, forming long, red, glistening stalactites. They hung there in the deep silence, ugly evidence of monstrous death struggles. I had lived through the war, had shot at and been shot at, and had seen war in all its ugliness, but this was the worst scene I had ever seen. I stood glued to the terrible sight, unable to move, nauseated. After a while, I slowly turned around and left. I had hoped that we could sleep in the barn that night, but instead we slept in the busses.

The next morning, we went back to work, stiff as boards. When the tide was about to change, we once again tossed in the bags and once again we saw most of them being dragged away by the sea. On and on, we tossed and when the water slowed down to a near standstill before changing direction, the gap once again began to narrow. It was a race against time, throwing bags in as fast as we could in the hope of closing the gap before the surge of in- and outgoing water became too powerful. In the end we lost. A water engineer looked at us, standing high on top of the dike.

"You'll never close the last ten feet or so. That water is too strong."

He turned around and left, but promised to radio for a new supply of bags. He just about killed our enthusiasm. Who were we to know better, when that engineer gave his verdict? We talked about what to do next, until one of the students decided for us.

"Listen, we have nothing else to do anyway. We might as well give it one more try." We began filling the bags again.

We had a visitor. A truck from one of the Dutch radio stations drove up and a figure, dressed in an ankle-long fur coat, approached us. A black Russian cap, drawn deep down his forehead, and the turned-up collar left only a mouth, nose, and eyes visible. The mouth was partially hidden behind a microphone. The figure introduced itself as a reporter from the BBC.

"I say, would you mind if I asked a few questions? Where are you chaps from and what are you doing here?"

I explained that we were students from the University of Amsterdam and that we were trying to close the break in the dike.

"Oh, how interesting. This is all very exciting, isn't it?"

He began describing the scene into the microphone. Only he made the break in the dike much larger than it was at that moment, the waves didn't lap over the remaining dike, the tide no longer ate huge chunks of dike away and there was no rain pelting down our faces. He was right about two things though—it was damned cold, and we were mud-splattered.

"I am standing next to a captain of the Dutch army, the leader of the group. Your name please, sir, and what do you study?"

223

I gave my name, adding that I was a medical student. "Aren't you afraid that this work will hurt your hands, seeing that you want to become a surgeon?" "This is hardly the time to think of one's hands, is it?" I walked away before my anger showed.

Unperturbed, he continued, "There you have it, ladies and gentlemen. Young men in an heroic battle, fighting to save a dike somewhere in flood ravaged Zeeland." The whole episode was a ridiculous break in the action.

Three hours after the engineer had given us the downer, an American plane came flying in low over the dike. From a large opening in the back of the plane, two men threw out bundles of empty bags, which the wind, coming from the side, blew in the sea. Slowly, the big plane turned around for a second try. I ran up the dike with an empty bag in each out-stretched hand and tried to direct the pilot, just like I had seen it done in a movie of aircraft carriers in action during the war in the Pacific. This time the plane came over without dropping bags, but a figure in the open door waved as it thundered over our heads. Again it turned around in a wide circle and the pilot maneuvered, carefully following the movements of my arms. When I thought that the plane was at the right angle to the wind, I dropped my arms and down came the bundles. Some still missed the narrow dike, but most landed safely and we had enough bags for the next twenty-four hours.

Two dark figures stood on the dike. I saw the black clothes and the black cap of the Zeeland farmer silhouetted against the sky as I looked up from down below. I walked up to them.

"You have any idea how we can fill that last gap?"

The taller one of the two shrugged. "We are farmers, not dike builders. We probably know as much about it as you do."

The smaller one just stared at the water, his eyes dull in a blank expression. Misery showed.

"You own that farm?" I pointed to the farm at the end of

the side road.

"Yep," the tall one said.

"Seen the cows?"

"Aye." He nodded. He had lost everything, his land, his prized cattle, his belongings.

"Wife and kids are safe," he said. "And I managed to get the bull and Bertha out."

"Bertha?"

"Champion cow, she is." Pride shone through the misery.

"I'm sorry."

There wasn't much else I could say.

"We've been trying to close the gap, but we need something real heavy to sink into it when the tide changes."

"Aye," he said.

They walked away in the direction of the farm. After a while, they came back, pulling a wagon and on it lay the linen chest from the flooded room in the farm. Solid, heavy oak, beautiful carved, seventeenth century, inherited from mother to oldest daughter.

"The wife's," he said.

We filled the chest and the wagon with bags and waited for the tide to change. When it did, they helped us push the wagon into the gap and then, working like men obsessed, we threw the bags in the water behind it. More and more, faster and faster, and then the first bags no longer disappeared below the surface.

"We got it," someone yelled.

Hundreds, thousands of bags.

Our improvised dam held and we built behind it until we felt sure that she would hold through the night. The next morning, it was still intact and we only had to reinforce our work. The engineer came by again and he couldn't believe his eyes.

225

"I'll be damned. Never would have believed it." He could start his pumps.

We looked at it for a while, exhausted. Not much was said. No hurrahs—too tired to enjoy. They were waiting for us in Middelburg with a warm meal and hot chocolate. A simple handshake and we drove the long way back to Amsterdam. The tunnel in Antwerp was dry. At the University, there was no one to welcome us.

"I'll see you," we said as we drifted apart.

At home, I took my boots off and dropped in bed for dead. When Nienke came home, she kissed five days of beard stubble and pulled a blanket over a mud spattered, unconscious man. In Zeeland, a farmwoman cried over the loss of a two hundred-year-old chest, a permanent piece in a dike.

The final death toll reached 1,835. Stavenisse, a village on the island Tholen, was worse off with 11.5 percent of its population drowned, 200 of 1,737. Over 72,000 people were evacuated, 40,000 houses were totally destroyed or severely damaged. More than 25,000 cows drowned, 1,500 horses, half the hog stock, and millions of chickens floated in the waters. The worst flood in Holland's history brought out the best of twenty-five nations. Five thousand American troops rolled in with massive material, driving tanks into the breaches to stem the surging waters, flying in box cars filled with food, clothing and sandbags. France sent two thousand pontoneers. One hundred and fifty Italian firemen arrived. England and Belgium sent rescue teams and their helicopters picked numerous women and children from the housetops. The details of the wretchedness gave evidence of the human drama that occurred during those first few days of the flood. A hastily put together raft carrying six people began to fall apart and one after the other they disappeared in the deep water. A farmer came in carrying his dead daughter. "The other one is also dead," he said. "Could carry only this one."

A family with four children hung on desperately from the roof of a barn. Icy wind and cold water numbed their fingers and one after the other, they let go until the last one slipped away. On a neighboring island, a man saw his wife and twelve children drown.

The ice cold water ironically saved two lives. A farmer and his wife fled to the roof. With one hand he held on to the chimney, with the other he held his wife. The waves slammed his right foot against the gutter, all night, all day and the next night. He hung on and when they were finally saved, they found the bones in his foot splintered. Only the farmer never felt it. The cold had acted as an anesthetic.

On an attic a doctor assisted a woman with the delivery of her first child. In the afternoon, mother and baby were swept under the ruins of her collapsing house. The sea made no distinction between the living and the dead. On a grave yard only the top of a head stone stood barely above the water. "Here rests Gerrit Jan Bossers" it reads.

You know, the Dutch can take land from the sea, but when the sea strikes back, we pay dearly."

The sisters never interrupted and remained silent when I finished.

Ann finally broke the silence. "That was another war."

"Yes it was," said Bets, "And you made us see it. Thank you. Those poor cows, and what must the farmer have felt."

This was to be the last time that I saw Bets; she died a few years later at age 82.

17

A Goal Reached

"I have news for you," Nienke said when I came home late one evening. "There is a mister Spruit."

"What do you mean, there is a Mr. Spruit? We have lived here for six months and Ms. Spruit never mentioned that she was married."

"Well she is, and her husband will come home tomorrow. He had been on a long business trip."

Mr. Spruit turned out to be an amicable, smooth talking man who could tell one joke after another. While his wife worked as a practical nurse in an old folk's home, he went looking for a job, which seemed to be very difficult for a man with his experience. He was an accountant. Once a month he paid us a visit to collect the rent and entertain us with his one of his many stories.

Friday morning, Nienke was at her office and I had my nose in the books, when I heard a loud banging on the door.

"Open up, police."

I opened the door and was immediately shoved aside by a burly fellow in a long raincoat. He waved some papers in my face and turned to two men behind him.

"Okay, fellows, move the stuff out."

"Just a minute. What is going on here?" I protested.

"Mister, we're throwing you out of the apartment. This here is a court order telling you to be out by two o'clock this afternoon. It's two by my watch if you know what I mean, so out you go."

"Over my dead body." I was hopping mad.

"Max," the man called over his shoulder.

A big policeman came forward.

"You tell him."

"Sir, this man is a process server," the policeman said politely. "You have not paid your rent and the court has issued an order for your eviction."

"What do you mean I haven't paid my rent? We have paid every month like clock work and I can show you the receipts."

I began to feel better. I was within my rights, at least I thought I was.

"Is your name Spruit?" the cop asked.

"No. See. You have the wrong man. We leased from Mr. Spruit."

"It don't matter who you are," the burly fellow budded in. "This here court order applies to all inhabitants."

"I'm afraid he is right, sir. You have to go." The cop was sympathetic.

Mr. Spruit's long business trip turned out to be a visit to the jail for embezzlement. Paying the rent had been my responsibility. When we moved to Amsterdam, I had taken a paper route. After four every afternoon, I walked the route with a bag over my shoulder, up and down the steps of the apartment complexes in Amsterdam South.

I called Nienke.

"You better come home. They're throwing us out of the apartment."

"What? How can that be?"

"Nien, please don't ask questions, just come over."

I quickly filled her in when she came home.

"Here ma'am, let me help you with these glasses."

The policeman came forward when she started to pack

the glassware. "I used to work in the moving business before I joined the police force. Let me show you how to pack them glasses." With his big hands, he tenderly took the wineglasses, wrapped them individually in newspaper and stacked them in a box. Nienke made hot chocolate for everybody and while drinking, the cop and the process server, who turned out to be human after all, told stories how an eviction sometimes became real ugly, especially when it concerned a lone woman and the neighbors sided with her.

The owner of the apartment—he owned the entire block of apartment buildings and then some—came to see for himself how things were going. He was a big man, easily three hundred pounds. His red face and nose were filigreed with fine blue veins. He was out of breath from climbing the three flights of stairs. He ignored us and turned to the process server.

"How is it coming?" he said in a surprisingly high voice for a big man.

"We are nearly finished." The process server motioned to us. "These people were sub-leasing and they paid their rent on time. Spruit kept the money for himself."

"That figures for a guy with his record," the owner grumbled.

Since the eviction was going to cost us, I decided to get some back from the owner.

"What about that wash basin?" I asked.

"What about it?" the owner said.

"That basin cost me two hundred and sixty guilders to have it installed."

"So?"

"So, either reimburse me or I'll rip it off the wall."

"Can he do that?" He turned to the cop.

"He sure can. It's his property, ain't it?" The officer was clearly on our side.

"Well, all right, I'll give you two hundred for it." He peeled two one hundred bills from the thickest wad I had ever seen before. It paid for the moving van.

———

We moved in with Nienke's parents and on February 10, 1955, she gave birth to our son Frank.

My study continued on track. Professor Borst, Chairman of Internal Medicine, was my favorite professor. He jogged before it was called jogging. The university hospital dated back to the sixteenth century and had no elevators. Medicine was housed on the third floors of two buildings that were connected by a corridor at each level, female patients in building A and the males in building B. When Borst, who was about sixty years old, made his morning rounds, he directed his much younger staff to use the corridor, while he ran down three flights and up again on the other side.

Borst was the only person, other than the Queen, for whom all traffic was stopped on the Spui, the busiest street in Amsterdam, only for him it was done every day. The police officer, who, with the aid of a 'Stop' and 'Go' sign directed the morning hour traffic at the crossing leading to the hospital, had been a patient of Borst's. Just before eight each morning, he was on the lookout and when he saw his professor come racing down the side street on his bike, with coat tails flapping in the wind like the wings of a large bird trying to take off from the water, the officer quickly turned his sign to 'Go' for him and Borst sailed across the intersection with a wave to his favorite cop.

Borst was not only a superb researcher on the topic of renal failure, he was also an inspiring teacher. He gave his most important lectures on Saturday morning from eight to ten. At ten, he paused for a minute, giving students a chance to leave, and then continued, freelancing with those who stayed. That was the finest hour. At the end of two years, he gave a final written doctoral exam and if you achieved a certain grade or higher, that was it. If not, he called you in for an oral exam as well. I knew I had done well on the written part and was therefore surprised when he called me in anyway.

"Sit down, please. I like to talk to you."

While he rummaged through a stack of papers, I looked around the old room with its magnificent woodwork. The bookshelves sagged in the middle under the weight of numerous books. Cows must have donated the leather of two easy chairs centuries ago. The floors were made of eight-inch wide boards, worn down in the path leading from the door to the desk. Dad would love to see the ornate ceiling with the trumpeting elves, I thought. Professor came to the point.

"You are older than the other students. How old are you?"

"Thirty-one, sir."

"Hmm. Start late?"

"No, professor. I began in 1942, but—"

"The war, eh? Started over again in—let's see—that must have been in 1949. Why so late?"

"First the underground and then five years in the army."

"Hmm. What are you interested in now that you finished your doctoral?"

"Professor, I'm a married man and we have a child. I have some catching up to do and I think I have a better chance to do that in America. I have applied for a visa."

He smiled and thought for a while. "Maybe I can help you."

And he did. It was through him that Professor Snapper offered to sponsor me for a rotating internship in Beth-El Hospital in Brooklyn, New York. Borst, the gray haired dynamo, was also the first person to show me that there was more to medicine than surgery.

On December 31, 1955, a tearful Nienke waved me good bye and I was on my way to New York City, where I would arrive thirty-six hours later. Halfway across the Atlantic Ocean, one of the engines caught fire. It was quickly put out, but after consulting with Amsterdam, the captain decided to turn back. They gave each passenger a room in the Amstel Hotel, but before taking a nap I called Nienke.

"Oh good, you arrived safely," she said cheerfully.

"No, I'm back in Amsterdam."

"They didn't let you in?" She was alarmed.

In small print, a warning at the bottom of my visa read, 'The United States Government reserves the right to deny the holder of this visa entry into the country at all times.' We had all read it. I explained what had happened and she came to Amsterdam to join me for a few hours. Fifteen months later, she followed me to America with our son Frank. A year later, I sold the family pride—the microscope—to Professor Louis R. Wasserman, Chairman of the Hematology Department of The Mount Sinai Hospital.

"You look tired," he said one day after rounds.

Of course I was tired. Every morning at five, I left our apartment in Yonkers to take the train to 125th street in Harlem and then with the subway to 102nd street. I walked the three blocks to Sinai and drew blood from all private patients before morning rounds started at eight. Evening rounds finished around eight-thirty, and I had night duty every third day. And I was tired of sleeping on a mattress on the floor next to the single bed, which Nienke used.

Doctor Wasserman grinned when I told him about the mattress.

"You got anything to sell?"

"Only my microscope."

"What kind of scope is it."

"A monocular Leitz from before the war."

The Leitz factories were behind the iron curtain and it was difficult to get a scope with good lenses.

"I'll give you two hundred dollars for it."

We attached a camera to the scope and she served us well in the making of beautiful pictures of blood cells. Nienke and I bought a bed. The Leitz, still complete with the light wooded carrying case, our family pride, had done its last service.

———

233

In 1979, I was invited to give a lecture on the treatment of childhood leukemia at the seventieth anniversary of the Dutch Pediatric Society. Professor van Creveld was my host. I had come a long way and was proud to give a talk in the old building and in Dutch no less. But that didn't last very long. The chairman of the meeting interrupted me after a few minutes.

"Professor, we appreciate that you want to give your talk in Dutch, but could you please do it in English?"

That was pretty humbling. My Dutch was no longer good enough.

I also paid a visit to Professor Borst, but his secretary wouldn't let me in to see him. She was drinking coffee with his senior assistants, who paid me no attention.

"The professor is much too busy to see sudden visitors. You must make an appointment a week in advance," she said, rather haughty, and continued her conversation with the assistants.

"Perhaps you'll be kind enough to tell professor that Professor Hoogstraten from America is here to see him."

That got her immediate attention.

"Certainly, professor." She left the room.

The assistants, a bit more respectful, smiled.

The secretary came back. "Professor will see you now."

Borst, now seventy years old, was still a spry man.

"I see from the program that you made it," he said and we had a nice conversation.

From my sister-in-law, I learned that Ann Frank now lived around the corner from her street and I went to see her. Mrs. Visser, her live-in caretaker, opened the door. I explained briefly who I was and asked her not to announce me. Instead, I went to the piano and played a little tune I had learned in 1943. As soon as she heard me play, Ann came rushing down from upstairs. "Barth, you're back!" Ann never forgot the touch of her students when they played the piano and she knew it was me by just hearing my fingers go over the keys.

Andy Tarnick with Antonia, his lovely Dutch wife

We sat together on the couch and had much to talk about. Bets died in 1969, and Ann bought a house on Hazel Tree Avenue, around the corner from where my wife grew up.

"Mrs. Stern came to see us with her two children," she said. "Her husband died in a concentration camp. She now lives in Israel."

Ann asked Mrs. Visser to go to the kitchen to make tea.

"Is she gone?" she said, making sure.

"Yes she is."

She felt for my hand and held it.

"We could have been lovers," she then said, quietly, still confident at eighty-nine years of age.

What could I say?

"Yes, Ann. We could have." It seemed the right thing to say. We were quiet for a moment.

"They took the tandem." Ann laughed.

"You must be kidding. The Germans took your bicycle?"

235

"Yes. We came driving back from the institute and two soldiers stopped us. They didn't care that I was blind. They just drove away with it."

I had heard that in their hurry to escape Holland, they had driven away in garbage trucks, but that really took the cake. We reminisced a while longer until Ann had to leave for a lesson. At her advanced age, she was still teaching.

I also paid a brief visit to Java Lane 4, to Mr. and Mrs. Van Dop. He was retired and recovering from a mild stroke, but the smile was still there and the cigar.

"Now tell me, did you and Nienke Adama get married?"

"Yes, sir, we did."

"I thought you two might get together. You helped her for the final exam, didn't you."

"Yes I did."

"As I recall, she finished in the top ten on the exam. All she needed was a good teacher." The smile, slightly crooked from the stroke, was finer than ever when he said that. Nothing had passed him by when it came to his students and he still remembered. How little does it take to make three grown people happy, I wondered.

"Well mother, do we have something under the cork for our visitor?" he said.

At Christmas time, 1996, I came across my old Ausweis and there on the back was the signature and address of Andy Tarnik, one of the American soldiers who had stayed with the Zierens after the liberation. I mentioned it to a friend, Chuck Henri, while playing golf and he immediately became enthusiastic.

"Canonsburg is only a couple of miles from where we lived. Why don't you find out whether he still lives there? That may be fun and he may like it."

I now also was curious and asked the telephone operator.

She confirmed that there was a Mr. A. J. Tarnik in Canonsburg, Pennsylvania and gave me the number.

"Are you Andrew J. Tarnik?" I said when a man answered the phone.

"Yes."

"And in 1944, did you sign an important document with your name and address?" "Who is this?" he said with a little suspicion in his voice.

"Well, I am the owner of that document and you were the American soldier who liberated me in 1944."

"What town was that?" he asked. "There were so many."

I explained and he remembered the house on Prins de Ligne Street.

"Now let me tell you something," he said. "I married a girl from there." Andy Tarnik had fallen in love with a girl from a small village next to Geleen and when the war was over, he returned to Holland to marry his Dutch sweetheart.

18

Five Years Under the German Boot

The Persecution of the Jews

Why did not more Jews survive the war? That question keeps coming back to me and I have yet to find a satisfactory answer. I have read many articles about it and discussed it with rabbis, but always it led to more questions. "Let it rest," the last rabbi suggested. "You will only uncover more dirt." In 1938, a Jewish student in my class, who I had helped a few times with homework, invited me for lunch with his parents. They had fled Germany two years earlier and spoke a mixture of Dutch and German.

"We want to thank you for helping Nathan. Today was his last day in school, because tomorrow we leave for America."

"America?" I was amazed. Not only did the mention of America surprise me, but also the suddenness of their leaving. "Why so sudden?"

"We know the Germans. Hitler will not be satisfied with just ruling the Fatherland. He will start a war, maybe bigger than the world war. He wants all of Europe."

Nathan's parents were wealthy. They had bought their way out of Germany and they, together with other wealthy German Jews, were not going to take another chance. Many

German Jews had found their way to Holland in the 1930's. In 1941, there were no less than 850 German Jews in Hilversum alone. The rich among them soon left for the Americas, but the less affluent stayed and waited. They knew what was coming and they warned us, but their warning fell on deaf ears.

The persecution of the Jews began slowly. It was as if the Nazis didn't want to alarm them and not upset the Dutch citizen. In October 1940, all civil servants, including teachers, were asked to complete and sign a simple questionnaire. It seemed innocent enough and so they all complied, but it included a question about their religion. One month later, on November 22, all Jewish civil servants were fired. They remained optimistic. Maybe it was only temporarily. Besides, this war wasn't going to last long.

As a next step the Germans requested that the Jews in the major cities form an advisory committee, a so-called Jewish Council. Of course the Jews obliged; what could be wrong with a council? And not surprisingly, the leadership of the council consisted of rabbis and prominent men. They were responsible for making a list of all Jews, as well as their addresses. The Germans treated these councils with some respect and politeness, and in turn the councils advised the Jews to register and do what the occupiers asked. Now all the Nazis needed was an excuse to round them up. For this they turned to their Dutch loyal counterparts, who were only too happy to assist in provoking the Jews. They began to yell and scream at them and soon they used their belts to beat them.

On Tuesday, February 25, 1941, the workers of Amsterdam had enough of the ever-increasing oppression of the Jews and went on strike. It soon spread to Zaandam just North of Amsterdam and to Hilversum, where that evening more than 10,000 people demonstrated silently in front of our town hall, where they confronted the SS. This action came

239

as a total surprise to the Germans, who somehow had assumed that the Dutch didn't care much for the Jews. They reacted immediately and ruthlessly. Gatherings of more than three persons were forbidden and would be met with summary justice. Strikers were subject to fifteen years imprisonment and for those working in factories that made products for the army, it could mean death. This resulted in nine deaths and two dozen seriously wounded. In Hilversum they set up machine gun posts at street corners and patrolled the town with armored cars and on foot. Two bombers from the airport nearby circled menacingly low over the center of town. In addition the German army commander imposed heavy fines on the citizens of the three towns.

By now it was obvious that the Nazis meant business as far as the Jew were concerned. They ordered the internment of all Jews and the Jewish Councils assisted in the selection of the first groups. The internment camp turned out to be the notorious camp Westerborg, a transit station to the extermination camps in Germany. Of the 120,000 Dutch Jews, a hundred thousand died in the gas chambers. Of 2,200 Jews living in Hilversum in 1940, more than two thousand went and died. It made no difference whether they were young or old. Ida Vos wrote a simple poem about a Jewish girl:

That last day in school she failed geography.
A week later, she knew exactly where Treblinka was.
But only for a day.

Why did so many Jews go like lambs to be slaughtered? Why did they not resist as the Jews of Warsaw did? Why did not more go underground when the opportunity was offered? My grandmother had a Jewish woman in her house. For three years, my uncle in Kortenhoef hid a Jewish family of three in his small house. Mother took a Jewish boy in for a while until she became too ill. And these are just examples of what one family could do. So there were many families, all ready to put their lives on the line, without hesitation. Some were motivated by their religion, others by a sense of duty, all because it was the human thing to do for their fellow Dutchmen. I will never get complete answers to these questions that stayed with me all these years. But I did find part of the answer in the action of our family physician.

Salomon Zwaap was born in Amsterdam on January 31, 1906, the son of Levie Zwaap and Roosje Goudsmit. He married a wellknown coloratura singer, the beautiful Esther Philipse, and they had two children. After completing his medical studies, he opened a practice in Hilversum and my mother was one of his first patients. He was a youngish looking man with fiery red hair just like mine. A warm feeling man with a strong personality, Dr. Zwaap became a pillar of strength for the Jewish community during the war. When the Nazis ordered all Jews to wear the Star of David, everybody advised him not to do so, but the Zwaaps wore the Star with dignity.

When the Jews were ordered to report for internment in a camp, he came to say a last goodbye to mother.

"You know you don't have to go, do you," Mother told him. "We and others will give you and your family a safe hiding place."

"Thank you Mrs. Hoogstraten, but I must go," he said quietly. "My people may need me," and he went. On December 11, 1942, the Chief of Police of Hilversum reported that the family Zwaap had been arrested by the SD and deported. The SD, or Sicherheitsdienst, was an arm of the SS and responsible for internal security and the elimination of the Jews. The SD and the Gestapo matched each other in brutality. Both were made up of misfits and dregs of society into which similar worthless characters from the occupied countries were recruited.

Dr. Zwaap made the greatest offer a doctor can make, his life, but he didn't only go as a physician. He also went as a

Jew, with pride in his people and a deep feeling of destiny. His wife and children followed him with confidence, without raising a question. Judaism teaches that no man shall separate himself from his community, and Dr. Zwaap, a deeply religious man, wished to stay with his community of Jews to better overcome the evil of the Nazis. The Zwaaps went and in so doing became part of Jewish history.

The Dutch Civil Registry is unbelievably thorough and so today we read under number 372 the following entry in the Registry of Hilversum:

"Today, May 8, 1951, I report as official of the Civil Registry of Hilversum, that based on a report from the Ministry of Justice, on October 1, 1944, died in Auschwitz, Polen:

Zwaap, Salomon, age 38, no occupation, born in Amsterdam, lived in Hilversum."

No occupation. It cries.

The baby survived

When the order came for all Jews to report to the SD in Amsterdam, the desperate parents of a seven months old baby asked a friend to safe the little girl. She became a bright light in the life of her surrogate family. That family was deeply involved in the resistance movement and the father had already died in a concentration camp. The mother and her two daughters continued their underground work and now also took the baby for safekeeping. "Our niece from Amsterdam is staying with us" they told the neighbors, who believed them or pretended to believe, because everybody loved Renee. Children in the street took turns pushing the baby carriage. She took her first steps on her first birthday, in March 1943 and fell in the arms of her 'mother'. Three months later the SD raided the house and in their eagerness they found another Jewish girl. Then they saw the happily smiling Renee. "That's another Jew bitch," they said. "Oh, no. She is our own niece," mother said and she took Renee in her arms. The SD'ers believed and left with their 'catch'.

'Mother' quickly put Renee in her carriage with extra clothes. "Take her away from here," she said to her own daughter Willy, "And don't come back." Willy left as fast as she could and had hardly turn the corner of the street, when the two SD men returned. "We want that baby or we'll arrest everyone," they said. 'Mother' was faced with a terrible choice. Could she or one of her daughters resist the torture for which the Gestapo was famous? Or would one of them succumb and give the names of other members of the underground? Or should she give up the baby?

"Ine," she said, "Find Willy and bring the baby back."

Renee and the other girl were moved to an assembly point in Amsterdam. Renee landed in the nursery, waiting for transport to Treblinka, the German extermination camp in Poland. 'Mother' immediately went to a lady in a nearby town and told her about Renee. "I'll see what I can do," the lady said. A few days later she called 'mother', "Come and pick up the baby." Helping hands had somehow smuggled Renee out of the nursery. Renee survived the war and had two daughters of her own.

The Partisans

The partisans were the armed men and women of the resistance. They were the ones who committed sabotage, liberated important prisoners, raided distribution offices and police stations, assisted the allied forces in various ways, executed a few highly undesirable individuals such as Polizeiführer Rauter, performed espionage and other tasks that needed to be done at the spur of the moment. A few examples of their activities in and around Hilversum come to mind.

On November 8, 1944, a message from Radio Orange in London came through: "We will also survive this winter." It

243

was a code to mean that at 7.30 PM the railroads in the center of Holland were to be sabotaged in 48 different places. Ge Verheul, a prominent partisan figure in Hilversum who worked under the pseudonym G 1, called his group of ten together in their headquarter S.25, and led them towards the railroad tracks between Hilversum and Utrecht. They crept through barbed wire, found their way through the anti-tank ditch and crawled on their stomach up the bank of the track. Two men placed the first charge, while the others stayed at both sides of the bank, ready for a surprise attack from a German patrol. They placed three explosive charges, three hundred feet apart. When they were nearly finished with the third, they heard a patrol approaching. In their haste to complete their work, they left some pins behind. They slid down the bank and pulled back into the shadow of the trees. When they reached their bikes, an enormous explosion lit the sky, followed by two others. About three hundred yards of railroad was destroyed, one of forty-eight.

Hilversum was the main telephone center for the German army. The town not only housed all Dutch radio stations, but also manufactured all signal apparatus in Holland. There was a military airport at the edge of town; the town had excellent rail and road connections, and it was considered the Garden City of Amsterdam. No wonder that the German Army immediately established its headquarters in the most affluent part of town. It was also to serve as the communication center for all German troops at the entire Western front. They build an enormous command bunker and lived and behaved like kings. They confiscated the office of the Dutch Telephone Company (PTT) and converted it into a huge switchboard complex.

That office used to be occupied by Uncle Jan and he wasn't too happy that he had been kicked out. The Germans were well aware that the underground depended on the telephone to keep contact. They ordered Uncle Jan to put a metal pin in all connections that were not used for their purposes. This he did, however, he also took other pins home and filed them down to the point that they were no longer effective. Under the eyes of the German guard, who didn't understand what was going on, he replaced the pins with the shorter ones and the resistance once more had the use of the telephone. It worked until the Germans disconnected the current. Uncle Jan, not to be discouraged, built a small switchboard in an empty factory in a street nearby. He borrowed a PTT uniform and cap, and under the eyes of curious Germans and police, started digging outside the German communication center. He tapped the main cable, made a connection for his own switchboard, closed the hole neatly and said goodbye to his audience. The resistance movement was back in business.

The illegal press kept up the spirit and hope of the Dutch people, that spirit the Germans tried to keep down at al costs. Several papers were produced in Hilversum, among them "Trouw" (faithfull), "de Waarheid" (the Truth) and "het Parool" (the Parole). J.W.Pel lived and worked on 16 Veerstraat. He was a printer and a widower with small children. He and a fellow printer, M. van Dijk, were responsible for the production of "Trouw". The distribution was in the hands of several co-workers and others were in charge of providing paper and ink. It was a large production and the coming and going of so many must have caused suspicion. Pel and three others were caught on March 20, 1944 and he died in a German concentration camp on March 13, 1945. Van Dijk was arrested in September and executed.

There are many others who braved the Nazis by keeping the common citizens informed. They paid with their lives. J.W.Oudenaller printed the "Free Gooi and Eemlander". He was arrested in February 1945, together with several co-workers. He assumed the guilt of the others and was executed. His friends survived. The printer of "De Gooische Koerier" was H. van Gangelen. He was caught in January, 1945 and shot on February 4. Four died in Hilversum because they believed, because they felt a duty. Just how many working with the illegal press died in the entire country?

In May 1943, the Germans ordered the handing in of all radios and this created the need for a separate paper for the illegal front. It would report important national and international news. Several listening posts gathered this news and the name of the paper was VOD, short for information service. The center of the resistance movement in Hilversum was U-61, a large villa on Utrechtse Weg 61. It was the rectory of the Reformed Church and the living quarter for its minister, Mr. Roth. With the permission of the church, he made the villa available as the center. Its leader was the pipe smoking Jan Stroes and sometimes as many as sixty people worked in Club U-61. Three members day and night manned the listening post of this center. Stroes put a team together to build a radio sender capable of sending and receiving messages from London. In 1942, Hilversum became the leading station in the region. It was fed information from around the country and passed it on to London. The sender was housed in hotel-restaurant "Het Hof van Holland", the favorite hangout of the senior German staff. Mr. Sprenger, the director of the hotel, had a dog, a huge German shepherd. That dog stayed in front of the door of the room housing the sender and the dog only moved when his boss called. The Germans thought that the operators of the sender were hotel personnel and the real personnel didn't know better then that they were electricians. One day, a friendly German warned Sprenger that the place would be raided in a few hours. The main wireless operator, van den Hul, managed to dismantle and hide most of the sender. When the Germans came and found the rest of the equipment, he confessed to listening to Radio Orange. They believed him. He was taken prisoner and died shortly after liberation day from the endured misery. The sender was rebuild and placed in a church. Most of the allied bombardments in Holland after 1942, were the result of information sent by Stroes and his staff. Members of an elaborate espionage network gathered that information. The network was known as "Albrecht", a young Dutch officer, who on July 16, 1942 left Holland and via Belgium, France, Spain, Portugal, Curacao and New York finally arrived in Bristol, England on November 27. He parachuted back in Holland on Friday, March 12, 1943 to assemble military information. He organized eight observation centers of which Hilversum and 'het Gooi' was one. In August 1944 the number of centers reached thirty and covered all occupied Holland. Albrecht tried to return to England with a load of microfilms, but he was arrested in the South of France on November 8, 1943. He was interrogated and tortured. He escaped, was wounded by a German patrol and again taken prisoner. But he survived and was liberated in 1945.

The leader of center Hilversum-het Gooi was T.J. de Geus, who worked under the name Arend. He operated from U-61 and traveled on his bike hundreds of miles each week throughout his territory. He drew extensive maps of the airport, of German command posts and other military installations. These, together with detailed notes, were brought to Utrecht by his courier, Dorus, again a pseudonym. The Germans caught her red-handed with a map and notes. They put her in a police station and began an interrogation supported by their favorite torture instrument, thumb screws. Dorus knew many contacts and who knows whether she could withstand the torture. The partisans decided to free her using firearms if necessary. Day and night they patrolled around the station waiting for an opening. Finally the door of the police station opened and a German guard appeared with Dorus. Three men on their bikes raced forward. Diest fired at the legs of the German and yelled for Dorus to jump on the back of bike of Willem. He kept the German at bay to

247

give Willem a head start, then piggybacked with Joop and off they sped away, followed by the several Germans on foot. At the corner, Joop lost control of his bike and down they went. Diest was hit in his leg, but he managed to reach his hiding place. A bullet hit Joop in his chest and lodged in his diaphragm. Losing blood and breathing with great difficulty, he stumbled to the house of a friend. With horse and wagon, hidden under a load of hay, he was brought to the hospital, bandaged, and with the same wagon transported to a safe house. Two days later, with his bullet still in place, he reached U-61 where he stayed for the rest of the war. Dorus and Willem reached their underground address safely.

Just how brutal could a German interrogation be? The German secret police were waiting for Dorus when she entered a house on Pieter de Hoogh Avenue, where every day she collected her messages. Mrs. Wolf, the owner of the house, was already in their custody and moved to a place in Loosdrecht. They knew that her two sons were in the resistance and they tortured her in a terrible way. But she never said a word. In the end they let a human wreck go free, knowing that it would soon die. And she did.

Arend continued his espionage work and ultimately made 17 drawings and submitted 81 reports. He also requested some key bombardments. In March 1945, the command bunker of the German Headquarters was hit leading to German deaths and wounded, as well as extensive fires. English fighter planes attacked ammunition ships in the harbor. On November 23, 1944, he observed a column of 15 tanks and many trucks and followed from a distance. They arrived in the Palm barracks and two days later the place was bombarded. In May 1944 a sketch of a strange airplane was sent to England. It was the first drawing the new secret German jet fighter. After the war, Arend, once again known as T.J. de Geus, stayed on in the military and ultimately became the Inspector General of the army.

Assisting the onderduikers

On February 9, 1945, Jan Jannsen, 29 years old and Gerrit van Wetering, 34 years old were put against a cold wall of the townhall of Zaandam and killed by a German firing squad. What major crime did these two citizens of Hilversum commit that they were condemned to die? One needs to go back to 1941 in order to understand what these two heroes of the resistance had done.

The first people to feel the effect of the food shortage were the families of navy men and commercial seamen who were caught at sea when the war broke out. The Germans regarded these men as enemy of the Reich and in 1941 ordered a drastic cut in the income of their families. They badly needed financial assistance, which soon began to arrive in the form of an illegal fund, the Zeemanspot, the Mariners Mug. This fund was initiated by a banker, Walraven van Hall, "Wallie" to his friends. Donations came in from all corners well in excess of millions of guilders, forcing van Hall to establish a disciplined underground organization with emphasis on secrecy and caution.

In the course of 1942, the number of people going underground grew dramatically and the illegal activities increased on an ever-greater scale. No only did the mariners wives need financial assistance, but also many 'onderduikers' and the men and women who worked full-time in the resistance. Money was also needed for the printing of illegal newspapers, for the production of false identity documents and for partisan activities. It was only logical that the leaders of the underground turned to van Hall for the nationwide organization of this effort. It became known as the National Support Fund or NSF under the leadership of Wallie, his brother Gijs and Iman van den Bosch, a director of the electrical giant Philips. These three men formed the "top" of the organization.

The NSF received a major boost when early in 1944 the Dutch Government in exile guaranteed repayment of all loans.

This really became a blessing when in September 1944 the government ordered a national railroad strike and 30,000 workers were suddenly without income. The money flowed in from small donations, from loans by banks and wealthy citizens, from churches asking for "donations for special needs", the meaning of which everybody understood. Civil workers of Hilversum authorized a secret deduction from their monthly pay for the NSF, which ultimately amounted to six million guilders. Anything was permitted as far as the NSF was concerned, even stealing. The directors and employees of the Central Bank managed to steal 51 million and workers of the IRS siphoned off a sizable amount for the NSF under the eyes of their Nazi bosses. At the end of the war the total contribution to the fund had reached 106 million guilders.

Collecting money was only part of the work. It also had to be distributed. But to whom? Who needed assistance most and how was the money to reach those people. The "top" realized that they had to have an army of trustworthy co-workers who could find those in need and determine what was needed. They divided the country into 23 districts and appointed a leader for each district, who in turn found a leader in each major city. Het Gooi was one of the districts and for Hilversum the leader became a lawyer, Jan Dirk Janssen, assisted by Gerrit van Wetering, the owner of a wellknown hardware store. The distribution of funds and food was the task of the women. They also became the couriers, because most men were either in Germany as slave labor or were underground during the last year of the war. The NSF, which eventually counted 1,800 men and women, distributed five million guilders each month.

The handling of the large amounts of money was kept as simple as possible. Every week the top financial man of the NSF collected two million guilders from five banks, but since his briefcase could only hold 1,000 notes of 100, he was forced to make five trips, on foot. The couriers stuffed the bags on both sides of their bikes with money and pedaled past German guards as if it was nothing. The recipients had to sign for the money and they did, using initials or pseudonyms. Jewish onderduikers did not sign. Ans Stellingwerf, one of the couriers, wrote in her diary: "March 31. Today I was on my bike from seven in the morning to eight at night delivering 40 packages for the resistance. I am dog tired." She did not mention that her bike had no tires.

Secrecy was a prime priority. The "top" only knew the 23 district leaders, but not the local leaders. And the local leaders in turn did not know the identity of the "top". Wallie especially insisted on strict disciple as far as secrecy was concerned.

How successful was this secrecy? Of the 1,800 workers "only" 85 were caught and executed. Sooner or later someone was arrested and then the Gestapo torturers went to work with their old and modern methods. Of those caught, most endured the worst torture imaginable without revealing the names of others. They were executed. But who can blame the person who couldn't stand the terrible pain any longer and in a moment of "weakness" blurted out a name, only to be executed any way?

On Saturday, January 20, 1945, two German members of the SD bolted into the home of Jan Jannsen. Before the Germans could grab him, his wife saw him quickly putting a piece of paper in his mouth and swallow. The news of his arrest spread like wildfire through Hilversum and although the SD remained in the house for several hours in the hope of catching someone else, they could not make another arrest.

Tuesday, January 23, at five o'clock in the afternoon, two men of the SD dressed in their hated black leather coats arrested Gerrit van Wetering at his home. Both Jannsen and van Wetering were interned in Amsterdam and repeatedly interrogated. Their mouths remained shut.

Walraven van Hall, Iman van den Bosch, Jan Janssen and Gerrit van Wetering belonged to the group of 85 NSF workers who lost their lives. Their crime was the giving of assistance to people in need, the oldest humane gesture. On Sunday, April 29, 1945, at 3:30 in the morning, Han, the wife of Jan Jannsen, gave birth to a son, Jan Diederik. A month later the baby died of infection; Han had lost both Big and Little Jan. After Holland was free, they found the body of Jan in a mass grave. On August 10, with full military honors, he was buried next to the son he never saw.

Epilogue

I last saw Ann in September 1990, when she was 100 years old. Through the front window of her house, I saw her sitting at the table, playing her wooden flute, the same flute I had practiced on. A young, aspiring social worker opened the door and showed me in. Inside the room, Mrs. Visser was about to greet me, but I motioned to her to keep silent. We listened to Ann play. The melody no longer came smoothly. There were many pauses for breath and it took a while before I could make out the melody of an old song I had heard her play many times before. When she finished playing, I took her hand. Years ago, she would have recognized my touch immediately, but now she was puzzled.

"Who are you?" she said.

"It's Barth, Ann."

"Barth? Barth? Do I know you."

She faced me, head tilted as always. But the eyes were no longer shiny, they now were truly the eyes of a blind person. Her once strong hand was frail, the skin thin as the wings of a butterfly, easily bruised, very soft. Slowly she felt my hand, the surface, fingers, palm.

"I know that hand," she said hesitantly. "But who are you? What is your name?"

She was an old lady, very old, very fragile. The vitality was gone, the laugh with the head movements never came during this visit.

"Do I know you?"

"This gentleman comes all the way from America to see you."

The young woman said it in too loud a voice, in the patronizing way that one tends to use with very old people. I mentioned that I had lived with her and Bets during the war.

"Bets was my sister."

"Yes, Ann, and I lived with you."

"Then I must know you. What is your name? Where was that?"

"That was in the house on Rembrandt Avenue, Ann," I said patiently.

Mrs. Visser dozed off on the couch.

"Oh, yes, Rembrandt Avenue. That's when Bets was still alive." She struggled to bring back long forgotten memories.

"Do you remember that we went to Geleen together?" I tried to help. "To Mr. Zieren, Cor Zieren."

"Cor?'

"Yes, we went to Mrs. Zieren's funeral."

"Cor was my husband."

And so we talked, painfully. "What is your name?" She said at least a dozen times. "Who are you?"

"I'll be back, Ann," I said after a while.

"That will be nice." She was polite, as to a stranger.

She was back in her blind world. Mrs. Visser had slid down the couch, snoring softly. Saliva drooled from the corner of her mouth. At first I felt disappointed. I would have liked to talk with Ann about my success in America, the professorship, of being of some importance in my field, of my family. But then I realized that there was nothing to tell. It would only have given me self-satisfaction and at that moment I wasn't important at all. Nobody, nothing is important when you are a hundred years old. She picked up the flute again and moved back into her world of music, her heaven on earth for a hundred years. Same old melody.

"It's really something, don't you think so, sir?" The young social worker said. "Her being able to play like that."

Ann Frank on her 100th birthday

How little did she know that these same fingers had once produced the most beautiful music, full of energy no longer there? Ann could not recall that Mrs. Stern had lived with us in the old house on Rembrandt Avenue.

"That I don't know anymore." Her voice, once so clear, was brittle. "How long ago was that? What is your name? Do I know you? I am a hundred years old."

She said it without feeling, without pride in her voice. The pride was taken over by the people around her. It was their hundred years. They dwelled on it.

"It's really something, isn't it, sir?" the young woman said again.

Mrs. Visser woke up as I stood to leave.

"Goodbye, Dr. Hoogstraten," she said. "Au revoir."

I softly kissed Ann on the head. She continued playing.

"Goodbye, sir," the young lady chimed as she let me out.

255

An empty feeling came over me as I slowly walked away, a lump in my throat.

"What is your name? Who are you?"

Ann's last questions stayed with me on the walk back home. It made me think of those thousands of men and women, who, without hesitation, had joined the resistance during the war and had paid the ultimate price. Who were they? People like Bernard IJzerdraat, who started the first illegal paper; Jan Compert, who wrote a poem just before he died; Gerrit van der Veen, who signed my false identity card and was executed. Walraven van Hall, a banker who organized a national effort to feed the families of onderduikers and seamen caught on the oceans when the war broke out. Jan Janssen and Gerrit van Wetering, two heroes who organized that effort in Hilversum. All three were betrayed and executed in February 1945. And the young woman, who became a courier and whose name we do not even know. People, like Bets and Ann, who took Jews into hiding, fed them and comforted them at enormous personal risks. Who were they? Now, so many years later, only one answer comes to mind—they were the best our country could give.

My sister-in-law sent me a copy of a lengthy September 22nd, 1990 newspaper article about the life of Ann Frank. It mentioned that her sister Riek's marriage name had been Stern and that she had a son Wouter Stern. Ten years later, Wouter and I had a long telephone conversation and I asked him if he had a brother. He did, Ernst Stern. Did he have a middle name, I asked. Yes, he said, it was Eduard. But Ernst was not born in Wageningen and not on the 15th of January 1927. So the two sisters had played a game with me fifty-seven years earlier when I needed a new name for my false identity papers. And they never told me why they had suggested that name, not even when we met again after the war. Two foxy ladies indeed.

Ann Frank died on June 10, 1992. She was 102 years old.

———